Young Families at Home

A Home Visitor's Guide
to the Young Family Parenting Information Books

Developed and Published by

219 North Second Street, Suite 200
Minneapolis, Minnesota 55401
612-332-7563

Staff
Victoria Hosch
Jacqueline Mosconi
Mary Nelson
Sue Letourneau
Sherry Wendelin

Consultants
Ann Walker Smalley
Raymond D. Kush

Cover art by Mary Beth Berg

©1999 Meld; 2003 Revised and Updated

ISBN: 0-9725011-8-5

Table of Contents

Table of Contents (continued)

Table of Contents (continued)

Home Visitor's Overview

Meld is parenting that works!

Meld has been making a positive difference in the lives of families for 30 years. A national non-profit education, training, and resource organization, Meld nurtures the crucial connections between parents and children by building skills, knowledge, support, and confidence.

By working with families in their home, practitioners are able to support parents as they bond with their child and nurture this most pivotal relationship in a child's life. Thank you for joining in this partnership with Meld on behalf of children and families.

Young Families at Home assists in "bringing home" timely and valued information for parents in the home setting. The guide assists home visitors in working effectively and respectfully with parents (either moms, dads, or both) from pregnancy through the first few years of their child's life. This guidebook is divided into sections that correspond to and build upon Meld's six-book series *The Young Family Parenting Information* books and facilitator guides for working with parents in groups.

The home visitor's guide includes

- hands-on, real-life learning activities
- valuable home visitor skill-building information
- time-tested tips for effectively working one-on-one with parents
- ideas for expanding and adapting materials (including prenatal, siblings, and more)
- enriching parent handouts
- additional background information for each topic

How This Guide Is Structured

In this Home Visitor's Overview, you will find information on how to structure a typcial home visit in Home Visit Framework. This is followed by guidelines for Home Visiting, which outlines basic concepts to know about how to approach home visiting.

The remainder of the guide is divided into six sections, each addressing basic information for parents of infants and toddlers. At the beginning of each section, information on the topic is provided to help the home visitor prepare for the visit. A list of concerns to watch for during a home visit is also provided. A home visitor may want to work with his or her supervisor in advance to decide how to respond to the concerns.

Each visit, then, has a format that is designed to support parents and relate to them on a personal level, as well as to provide valuable parenting information. It is presented in a "structured" way to guide the home visitor, knowing that the actual home visit will take on a more relaxed and informal feel. Parent handouts conclude each section, providing lasting resources for parents. You are encouraged to supplement these with specific resources from your community.

Home Visit Framework

Each home visit will be unique, but you can bring structure to the visits by including the following steps in each visit. The learning activities from *Young Families at Home* can be used during the information topic part of your visit. Depending on the family and the topic you will cover, your visit may include from one to three learning activities from the curriculum.

Opening

Greeting

- introductions (if needed)
- become familiar with environment, including noting home ground rules (taking shoes off, etc.)
- update on what's happened since last visit

Sharing Time

- casual conversation (spread throughout visit)

    - affirm parents
    - learn about the family's strengths and needs
    - build trust and relationship with family members
    - model positive interaction with children
    - share personal experience when appropriate
    - ask parents about what kinds of information or support they may be interested in receiving

        child's progress
        parent-child relationship
        personal concerns
        experiences with community resources

Keeping It Going: Information Topic

- ask the parents what they already know about the topic

- add additional information

- do learning activities

    - child development
    - parent-child activities
    - programs, services, and support available

- refer to the parent materials

    - community resource information

Closing

- summarize the visit

    - set goals to accomplish by the next visit and determine individual responsibility
    - set the date and describe the content of the next visit

Follow-up

- documentation

- complete agreed-upon tasks toward meeting goals

- collect information for the next visit

- consult with your supervisor as needed

Guidelines and Suggestions for Home Visiting

Home visiting is a service delivery strategy that is used in a growing number of family support programs. Research indicates that home visiting may be most effective when used in conjunction with other strategies that serve parents.

Recent research also suggests however, that for the most impact, family services must be provided when the children are very young. It is also evident that the home can be a rich learning environment. The home visitor supports parents one-on-one. Teaching and modeling care of young children is provided in a more realistic setting.

Parents are the first teachers of children and are usually the most important and consistent person in a child's life. Parents' own needs also must be met for them to best respond to their children. Family services are most effective when they aim to empower parents and act as partners with the family.

Home visiting can connect isolated families to the community and to the resources in that community. Families can request and receive information and feedback through home visits.

Home visitors develop their individual style to deliver the information and support they bring to parents. Each family will have its own way to receive and use the information and support. The ways in which these interact determine the effectiveness of the home visit. To make the interchange as useful as possible, keep in mind the following suggestions for home visits.

Suggestions to Help Home Visits

Don't take on the parents' responsibilities.

In an effort to be "helpful," it's very easy to do things that are really the parents' responsibility instead of helping the family grow and learn for itself. Even the most competent and experienced home visitor must watch for the tendency to assume responsibilities that belong to the parents.

Don't force one's own values upon the parents.

Everyone has a tendency to try to change others to the "best" way to do things, based on personal experience and/or expertise. Home visitors need to be able to share their own experiences with families without imposing their values upon families.

Be aware of the limits of friendship.

The relationship between the home visitor and the family must be friendly but not overstep the professional boundaries. Sometimes "friends" can take on each other's responsibilities and enable each other to engage in nonproductive behavior in the name of friendship.

Don't prescribe for the family.

When a home visitor diagnoses and prescribes a course of action for the family, we deprive the family of a valuable opportunity to learn how to assess its own needs and find ways to deal with them.

Don't generalize from one situation to another or stereotype.

Home visitors must constantly remind themselves that each family situation represents a unique combination of strengths and needs. What works well for one family may be totally inappropriate for another.

Be aware of taking on too much.

The needs of some families are so great that a home visitor may take on too much responsibility. Supervisors must help home visitors set appropriate limits and expectations.

Support the whole family.

Whenever possible, home visitors must involve all significant family members in the services provided. When that is not possible, the home visitor needs to consider these relationships in all his or her dealings with the primary client.

Present a full range of options.

Home visitors are obligated to be as thorough and creative as possible when asked to provide information on the alternatives available to a family. Families are best helped when they are made aware of the wide range of options available to them.

Don't let egos interfere.

Home visitors may at times be vulnerable to the "ego trip" that comes from helping families solve their problems. It can be very heady to know that you can help individuals deal with certain situations. Home visitors are not effective when they relate to families from a position of perceived superiority.

Don't expect change too quickly.

It is easy to lose sight of the fact that it can take a long time to change habits and behaviors that have been established for years. Expecting change too quickly can prove frustrating and self-defeating for all involved.

Be consistent.

Consistency—keeping appointments, following through with agencies, being a reliable source of information—is one of the most critical guidelines for home visiting. Families must be able to trust that the home visitor will come through for them as promised.

Consider all safety issues.

Home visitors must take adequate and reasonable precautions to ensure their personal safety. Talk with supervisors and coworkers about the best ways to stay safe during home visits in your community.

Keep knowledge and information up-to-date.

A sound basic knowledge of child development, parenting, and other relevant family life information is important. The ability to access other appropriate resources is a critical foundation for an effective home visitor.

Plan for separation or termination of relationship.

As strong and powerful bonds grow between the family and the home visitor, it can be easy to forget that your time together is limited. From the beginning, preparation for the end of the relationship should be built into the relationship.

Recognize when to stop.

Home visiting can sometimes create more problems in families than it can solve. When this happens, the home visitor must be able to recognize the situation and be willing to let go if that seems best for the family.

Maintain confidentiality.

Home visitors and the families develop close relationships in which much is shared. Families must know that what they tell the home visitor will be kept in professional confidence. Home visitors must also be clear with families about when and what may be necessary to share with others due to legal, ethical, or agency guidelines.

Be clear about mandated reporting.

Most families you will work with will be striving to do their best for their children. It is important however, for the home visitor to be aware of the obligations regarding mandated reporting of suspected maltreatment in his or her state. It is best to share your professional obligations with parents at the beginning of your relationship.

Chapter 1
Baby Is Here!

Introduction

Home Visitor Information

The purpose of *Baby Is Here!* is to help parents become comfortable taking care of their baby's basic needs in a loving way and to encourage parents to spend as much time as possible playing with their baby and getting to know her. By responding to their baby's needs and playing with her, parents (and their baby) develop a strong, loving attachment. Attachment is important because it is the foundation of the relationship between the parents and their child. Attachment gives a baby the security of love and the knowledge that there are people who care about her and will take care of her. Securely attached babies become more self-confident, curious, and better able to adjust to new situations, and they become ready to learn. The "Little Things Mean a Lot" activity has been added to help you help parents become more nurturing with their baby.

The "Having Fun with Baby" activities stimulate brain development, which recent research has shown as very important at this young age. A safe and stimulating environment offers experiences that help create "wiring" in a baby's brains. This wiring is what makes it possible for children to learn and grow throughout their lives. Encourage parents to show their love for their baby by giving him time and attention. Parents can help their babies develop by involving them in their day-to-day activities. Use your time with parents to model the types of behaviors and interactions that build trust and stimulate development.

The topics in *Baby Is Here!* focus on the early months of life with a baby. Even if a baby is older than five months, you can use the "Having Fun with Baby" section to help parents understand their baby and to get comfortable playing with her.

You may use this book with parents before their baby is born, too. In that case, you would focus the discussion and questions on getting ready for the baby and making some important decisions about feeding and diapering. You can support their decisions by giving them accurate information.

After the activities in *Baby Is Here!*, parents will

- know when their baby is hungry
- understand why they should hold their baby when feeding
- know the importance of burping their baby and how to do it
- know when their baby is full
- know how a mother can take care of herself if she is breastfeeding
- know how to breastfeed
- understand the issues that surround breastfeeding
- be able to decide between breast or bottle-feeding or a combination
- understand the different types of baby formula and which type is best for their baby
- decide what type of diaper (disposable or cloth) works best for their baby and for them
- learn how to diaper a baby
- understand the importance of keeping their baby clean and dry
- practice giving their baby a bath
- learn how to keep bathtime safe
- learn how to keep baby clean between baths
- understand that bathing their baby gives parents a chance to play with their baby
- understand why babies cry
- learn ways to soothe a crying baby
- learn ways to deal with their own feelings when their baby cries
- learn 20 rules for keeping their baby safe
- begin to understand their baby
- learn how to play with their infants and young children

Important Information for Home Visitors

- When parents feed their baby, they give food and love. The act of responding to their baby's need for food is one very important way parents show they care about their baby. Encourage parents to hold their baby and to look into his eyes and talk to him when feeding.

- Both breastfeeding and bottle-feeding will give a baby the nutrition he needs. The only food babies need until they are six months old is breast milk or formula.

- Hold a baby when feeding him. Never prop a bottle or put a baby to bed with a bottle.

- Parents should only use food to stop crying when their baby is hungry. Food should not be used to comfort all of a baby's cries.

- Both mothers and fathers can feed their baby. If a baby is breastfed, dad can give a bottle of expressed milk or burp the baby when she's finished eating.

- Feeding problems can be difficult for both parents and their baby. Parents may feel like they are not doing a good job if they are uncomfortable with the choices they have made about breastfeeding or bottle-feeding their baby. Other people may want to give parents advice about how to feed their baby. Parents need to listen and then decide what is best for themselves and their baby. If feeding problems do happen, parents will need support and encouragement as well as ideas for what to do about the problems.

- Keeping a baby clean helps her to stay healthy. Babies usually need a bath two or three times a week. A baby can get a diaper rash if diapers aren't changed often enough.

- A baby doesn't cry because she wants to make her parents mad. A baby cries to let other's know she needs something.

- When a baby cries, he needs comfort. A baby doesn't become spoiled if his cries are comforted. Responding to their baby with gentleness and love is one way parents and the baby develop a close attachment.

- Sometimes being a parent is hard. Parents can take care of themselves by eating good foods and getting enough rest. Parents benefit by taking time for fun, getting out of the house, and being with friends, too.

- When a baby keeps crying, parents can feel frustrated, worried, rejected, or very angry. Feeling mad is okay... most parents feel mad at some time. But expressing anger in dangerous ways is **not okay**. Parents can seriously hurt (and even kill) their baby if they hit, shake, slap, punch, or throw their baby.

- When parents start feeling very tired or angry, they need to make sure their baby is safe (leave the baby with a trusted adult or in a safe place) and then find a way to become calm. Parents need to ask someone for help or tell someone how they feel, either in person or on the phone. If possible, keep phone numbers of several people or places to call for support near the phone.

- Babies can't keep themselves safe—that's their parents' responsibility. Learning about possible dangers, childproofing, knowing where the baby is, and what she is doing at all times can prevent many accidents.

- Playing with a baby helps him learn and grow best. Playing helps a baby understand about himself, others, and the world around him. It also encourages brain development and learning.

- No two babies are alike. Each grows and learns at a different rate. Each has a unique personality, but each is wonderful and special.

- Parents learn how special their baby is and how different she is from other babies by playing with, watching, and taking care of their baby. When it comes to the important things about their baby, parents know their baby best.

Additional Topic Information

Breastfeeding

Each family needs to decide how to feed their baby. For some parents, this may be a hard choice to make. They may have some ideas about breastfeeding or bottle-feeding that aren't true. They may have family or friends who think they should do things a certain way. Parents may have a lot of questions about each way of feeding but are afraid to ask people who could answer their questions. You can help parents make the decision that is right for them by giving them accurate information and supporting their choice.

How to Feed a Baby

Parents can either breastfeed or bottle-feed their baby or use a combination of both. Either will give the baby the nutrition she needs. The important thing for parents to remember is that feeding time is more than just giving their baby food. When parents hold their baby close during feeding time, there are strong emotional and physical feelings for both the parents and the baby. This is a special time for parents and their child to be together, get to know each other better, and share love. When parents hold, cuddle, and talk to their baby during feeding, the baby feels love from the mother or father. This special time helps parents and their baby grow close to each other.

Parents can develop a close relationship with their baby whether they breastfeed or bottle-feed. It's important that both mother and father have the chance to hold and feed their baby. Then, both mother and father will be able to feel close to their baby. Dads can feed a breastfed baby a bottle of expressed breast milk or formula or he can participate in other ways.

You can help parents feel confident about feeding their baby. When you see parents who hold their baby close and gently when they feed, tell them they are doing a good job.

When to Feed a Baby

It can be hard for new parents to know if their baby is hungry, tired, upset, or bored when he cries. After parents get to know their baby better, they know if their baby is hungry by how he acts. Parents need to remember that it takes awhile to learn this.

If parents are not sure if their baby is getting enough to eat, there are some things they can do to figure it out. One is to count how many times the baby eats in 24 hours. As long as a baby eats six to eight times in 24 hours and the feedings are 2-1/2 to 5 hours apart, the baby should be okay.

Another way parents can know if their baby is getting enough to eat is to count how many wet diapers the baby has. If a baby has 6 to 10 wet diapers each day, then he is probably getting enough to eat. Parents can check to be sure their baby is gaining enough weight when they take him in for a checkup.

If parents still aren't sure if their baby is doing okay, encourage them to ask their health care provider about how the baby is doing during their next visit.

If parents are breastfeeding, they have a lot to learn and will probably need some help and a lot of support. If this is the first time they are breastfeeding, the mother will need to learn how to

- position the baby on the nipple
- know when one breast is empty and how to switch the baby to the other breast
- express milk
- take care of sore or engorged breasts

A breastfeeding mother must take good care of her own health so she can make enough quality milk for her baby.

Even if parents are not breastfeeding, it's important that they learn about it because someday they might breastfeed another baby.

Parents may have many kinds of questions and concerns. It may be difficult for the parents to openly discuss breastfeeding. The mom may be embarrassed to talk about it with you. Dad may feel uncomfortable just talking about breastfeeding. You can help them overcome some uncomfortable feelings. Your willingness to talk about breastfeeding will help them see that it's a natural and beautiful part of motherhood.

You can help parents through the first few months of feeding their baby by providing them with information about breastfeeding. If it just doesn't seem to work out for parents to breastfeed, you can help them decide whether to keep trying or to try bottle-feeding. If parents decide to bottle-feed, you can help them feel good about that choice and tell them that it doesn't mean they are not good parents if they aren't able to breastfeed their baby.

You can provide help and support to breastfeeding parents. You can listen to them, give them information, and offer support and encouragement.

Problems with Breastfeeding

When things aren't going well, both parents and baby can feel hurt, angry, and frustrated. The baby may be hungry but not able to get enough milk. The mother may be trying to feed, but does not know why her baby is having trouble eating.

If parents have accurate information, some feeding problems may be avoided and parents will know what to do if problems happen. Help parents think of where they can get information and support, such as their clinic or lactation consultant. Parents need to know how to feed their baby, when to feed their baby, and how to begin feeding. It's important that you talk about how to breastfeed **before** you talk about feeding problems.

Talking about feeding problems before they happen may help parents feel better when problems do happen. Having someone to talk to when a problem happens is very important. Parents need to remember that having problems with feeding **does not mean** that they're not "good" parents. Encourage parents to call you or their health care provider to find ways to solve breastfeeding problems. Encourage fathers to try to find out what kind of help they can give to mothers, too.

Bottle-feeding

If parents are bottle-feeding, they have a lot to learn, so they will probably need some help and a lot of support. If this is the first time they are bottle-feeding, parents will need to learn

- how to choose what kind of formula to use

- how to make formula

- how to feed their baby

- how to take care of bottles and nipples

Bottle-feeding parents must take good care of their health, too, so they are able to take good care of their baby. Even if parents are not bottle-feeding, it's important that they learn about it because they might bottle-feed another baby.

You can help parents through the first few months of feeding their baby by providing them with information about bottle-feeding. If parents need to try some new ideas for feeding their baby, you can give them the support and encouragement they need.

You can help parents feel confident about feeding their baby. When you see parents who hold their baby close and gently to feed, tell them they are doing a good job. If feeding problems develop, you can help think of solutions or encourage them to talk to their health care provider. You can provide help and support to bottle-feeding parents. You can listen to them, give them information, and offer support and encouragement.

Diapers

Think back to when you changed a diaper for the first time. Had you ever changed a diaper before? If you didn't know how to change a diaper, who showed you how? Were you afraid you might hurt the baby? Did you think that the diaper might fall off?

How did you make it a pleasant experience for the baby? Did you ever try to make the baby smile or laugh while you were changing the diaper? Did anything funny ever happen while you were changing a diaper?

It isn't always easy to change a baby's diaper. Babies can move around a lot. They wiggle and may try to reach for your face or hair or their toes. A baby may cry while the diaper is being changed. Sometimes the smell of a baby's urine or bowel movement is very strong. Parents may feel like they can't even change the diaper. Parents may feel bad about not wanting to do it.

If a baby has a diaper rash, he can cry even more during changing. When a baby has a diaper rash, parents can feel like it's the baby's fault or that they aren't doing a good job as parents.

Parents have to change diapers in all kinds of places: at home, at church, at a family member's home, at their clinic, while out shopping. Practice changing diapers so the parents can do it quickly and simply. Practice can make diapering a snap no matter where it's done.

The parents will have some of the same experiences with and feelings about diapering that you may have had. You can help parents feel confident about changing diapers. You can let them know when they're doing a good job. Once the parents feel confident, they will be able to learn how to make diaper changing a special time with their baby.

Changing a baby's diaper can be a time to look at and talk to the baby. Parents and their baby can even have fun! Babies like to be clean and dry. When a baby knows he is getting a clean diaper, he may become happy and playful. If parents remember that babies like to look at faces, they can make diaper changing fun for their baby by talking, singing, or making funny faces.

If parents have accurate information about changing diapers and can practice in a comfortable setting, some problems may be avoided and parents will be able to handle any problems that do happen.

Baths

Think back to when you gave a baby a bath for the first time. Were you scared? Were you afraid the baby would slip out of your hands or that you would get soap in the baby's eyes? Did anyone help you or show you how to give a bath to a baby? Who helped you?

Bathtime can be a very special time for both parents and their baby. Parents can talk or sing to their baby during a bath, they can learn more about their baby, and watch how he reacts to the feel of water or soap. As their baby grows, parents can see how she begins to play in the water. Their baby will feel love from her parents during bathtime. A baby likes to feel clean, be wrapped in a clean towel, and held close to her mother or father.

A baby may need time to get used to taking a bath. Other babies will like it from their very first bath. No matter how a baby reacts to her first bath, most babies like things to be the same each time. When things are the same, a baby knows what to expect. When bathtime is always the same, the baby will get used to it and can enjoy it. When parents do the same thing each time their baby has a bath, it is called a *bath routine.*

Some things that can be part of a bath routine are giving the baby a bath at the same time of day, washing the baby the same way each time (starting at the baby's cord, then head, then hair, then the rest of the body), or playing the same games or singing the same songs with the baby during a bath. As their baby gets older, parents can try some new things when giving a bath. When they find something their baby likes, they can make that part of the bath routine.

Parents need to be careful when giving their baby a bath, but they will become confident once they know how to give their baby a bath and see that their baby is enjoying it. Parents do need to remember that water can be dangerous. They must always check to see if the water is too hot before putting their baby into the water. They must **never** leave their baby alone in or near water.

Bathtime can be a very special time. Parents can show their baby how much they love him by handling him very gently, by holding him safely in the water, by making him feel clean and wonderful. These special moments are important. A baby learns to trust his parents. A baby and parents can share love. Mothers and fathers need to have this special time with their baby.

Help for a Crying Baby — How to Help

Think back to when you cared for a newborn. Did the baby cry a little? A lot? Did the baby ever cry for a **very** long time? How did it make you feel? Did you feel like you weren't a good caregiver because you couldn't help the baby stop crying?

How long did it take you to learn why the baby was crying? For example, when were you able to tell a "hungry" cry from a "tired" cry? What kinds of things did you do to comfort the baby? What did others tell you about comforting a crying baby?

Taking care of a crying baby is not always easy. When their baby cries, parents can feel mad or frustrated. Parents may not be able to find out why their baby is crying. They may feel like the baby is crying on purpose to make them mad.

One of the first things new parents need to understand is that **all** babies cry. Most babies cry at least 2-1/2 hours each day. Babies may cry when they are hungry, wet, uncomfortable, bored, scared, or lonely. Parents should also try to remember that when they were babies, they cried, too. Most likely, someone loved them enough to comfort them and find out what they needed.

Crying is a natural, necessary part of life. You can help parents understand that crying isn't something bad or something their baby does to upset them. Crying is actually something good. Some scientists have studied crying. They have found that people who cry are healthier than people who don't cry. Crying helps us to express our anger and frustration.

When their baby cries, parents need to find out why their baby is crying. Some people will say, "Let your baby cry it out," or "If you pick up your baby every time she cries, you will spoil her." Young babies **will not** become spoiled when parents comfort their cries. **Babies need to be comforted.** When parents comfort their crying baby, the baby learns to trust the parents. The baby feels love from her parents.

When you're visiting a family, how you deal with their crying baby can affect how parents react to a crying baby. If the baby cries and you get upset, the parents may also get upset. If you stay calm and help the parents to comfort their baby, they will learn how to comfort their baby and that it's okay for their baby to cry.

The parents probably will have some of the same experiences with and feelings about crying babies that you had. You can help parents feel confident about comforting their baby. You can let them know when they're doing a good job. Once parents feel confident, they will be able to learn why their baby is crying and how to comfort her. When parents have accurate information, they can learn to help their crying their baby and build a loving, trusting relationship with their baby.

Help for a Crying Baby — What Parents Feel

Each day, a baby cries. Sometimes she can cry for ten minutes. Sometimes she can cry longer than ten minutes. When their baby cries, parents need to try to find out why. Sometimes, no matter what parents do, their baby keeps on crying and crying.

Think back to when you first cared for an infant. Did the baby ever cry for a very long time? How long did the baby cry? How did that make you feel? What did you do? Did you find out what was making the baby cry? If not, what did you do?

It takes a lot of energy for parents to take care of their baby, especially when the baby is sick or when the baby is crying and the parents can't find out why.

You can find information about how to take care of a sick baby in the parenting information book *Healthy Child/Sick Child*. In this section, you try to help parents remember to take care of themselves and their baby when he cries.

This information about comforting a crying baby is very important. You may want to present it more than once. You may also want to check with the parents at each visit to see how things are going and if they are having problems. You can ask

- Are you taking care of yourselves?
- Are you getting enough rest?
- Are you taking time to do things you like to do?
- Are you taking time to have fun?
- Do you have someone who will listen to you when you talk about your feelings?

The best way for parents to help their crying baby is to be well-rested and relaxed so that, if their baby keeps crying, they will have enough energy to stay calm and not get worried or angry. All of us however, have our "breaking points" or "boiling points" when we get so tired or so angry that we do things that may hurt ourselves or others.

Sometimes parents are surprised at the feelings that they have when they're tired or frustrated. Strong feelings can lead to strong actions that can hurt the parent or their baby. Parents need to remember that, at some time, they will feel like they're "at the end of their rope." Before this happens, parents should have some ideas of what they can do so they are able to handle the situation. This will help them get through the hard times and know that their baby will be safe.

Some people have very quick tempers. They can get angry very quickly over things that may not seem very important (like misplacing something or finding out the store is out of their snack). Parents who have quick tempers need to find ways to deal with their anger so they don't hurt themselves or their baby.

There are ways to stop anger before we hurt ourselves or someone else. Most parents can control their anger by leaving the situation for awhile, trying to calm down, or calling someone to talk or get some help.

If parents reach the point where they may hurt their baby out of anger, there are some things they can do. Parents can

- put their baby in a safe place (like a crib or playpen) and go to another place in the house

- call or visit a friend, relative, or another parent to talk about what they are feeling

- ask a friend or relative to watch their baby for awhile so they can have a break

- take their baby to a crisis nursery where someone will watch the baby so they can get away for awhile

Once parents have talked about their feelings or had a little break from taking care of their baby, they usually feel better. Eventually, the baby will stop crying and parents will once again be able to take care of him.

You can help the parents cope with crying babies in two ways:

- You can remind them and encourage them to take good care of themselves. Encourage them to relax and have fun once in awhile. Let them know that it's okay to want to spend some time away from their baby.

- You can help parents understand and plan exactly what to do when their baby is crying and they reach their "boiling point."

If the parents have as much support and information as possible, it may be a little easier to make it through the times when it's hard to be a parent. When parents make it through the hard times, they'll feel even better about themselves and their baby. They'll be on their way to building strong, trusting, and loving family relationships.

Keeping Baby Safe

Where did you learn how to keep an infant safe? Did someone tell you? Did you learn some things "the hard way" when a baby had an accident?

Babies cannot keep themselves safe. Babies want to move around, touch things, put things in their mouths, and explore new places. Babies don't know what things are safe to do and what things aren't. Parents need to think about safety for their baby and keep him safe.

While parents may not be able to prevent all accidents from happening, there are many things they can do to keep their baby as safe as possible. One thing parents can do is to follow some simple safety rules with their baby. These rules, listed in the parenting information book, may seem like simple common sense, but it helps when they are spelled out.

Encourage parents to think about safety all the time. Parents are busy people and sometimes they forget to think about their babies. When parents aren't paying close attention to their baby, accidents can happen.

"Keeping Baby Safe" is a very important section that contains a lot of information. More information about safety can be found in the parenting information book *Safe Child and Emergencies*. That book also contains information about what parents can do if their child does have an accident.

Help parents keep safety uppermost in their minds. When you talk about how their baby grows, you can point out that, when children learn to crawl or walk, parents need to think about how these new skills will affect their child's safety. Ask questions about safety whenever you can.

Getting to Know Your Baby

Babies grow and develop starting at their head and finishing with their toes. First, they gain control of their heads, then their neck muscles, then their backs, and finally their legs and feet. All babies follow this same order, but not all do it at the same pace.

If you have children, think back to when your children were young babies. Did you keep any records of when your children learned to sit up, walk, or talk? Did you ever wonder about whether your babies were growing and developing okay? Did you talk to anyone about your worries?

What type of temperament did your children have when they were babies? Did your children have similar or very different temperaments?

What did you learn about how babies grow and develop from your own experiences as a parent? Did your children do the same things at the same age? For example, did your children each learn to sit up at the same age?

To grow best, babies need love, good food, plenty of sleep, clean diapers, a safe place to play, and lots of time with parents, loving caregivers, and other family members.

Each baby is special and grows at his own pace. Two babies who are the same age might be able to do very different things. One baby might be able to sit up alone. The other baby might be able to sit up and crawl. Two babies of the same age may have very different temperaments. One baby may be very active, may not cry very much, and be able to handle changes in his life easily. Another baby the same age may be very passive, cry more, and not like any changes.

Parents need to get to know their baby so they can help him grow the best he can. One of the most important things parents can do is stand back and watch their baby. What is the baby doing? Is the baby happy? What things make the baby happy? What things make the baby upset? How does the baby act when he is tired? When does he usually get tired? What things is the baby curious about? What does the baby like to play with? Help the parents do this during your visits. You can comment on what their baby is doing, what it means to develop, what might be coming next, and suggest ways to encourage development.

When parents get to know their baby, they feel closer to their baby and see how special their baby is. They will be able to help their baby grow and develop and will know if their baby is having a problem.

If parents have accurate information about growth and development, they can learn how to help their baby grow and also know when their baby might need special help. You can help parents feel confident in knowing their baby. You can let them know when they're doing a good job.

Baby Play

Think back to how you have played with babies. What kinds of things did they like to do? Maybe there were times when you didn't even know you were playing. When the baby dropped something over and over again for you to pick up, it may have been fun for your baby but seemed like work to you.

Play helps babies grow best. Play helps babies learn about themselves, others, and the world around them. It helps babies practice important skills they need to develop in a healthy way. For example, when a baby is learning how to reach out and grab something, she is developing eye-hand coordination, which eventually will help her to learn how to catch a ball, learn to write, and more.

Playing together helps parents and babies get to know each other and share love. Parents can teach their children important things about their culture through traditional songs and games.

Playing with babies encourages brain development, too. When parents play with their baby in different ways, different parts of their baby's brain get a "workout." All the games, funny faces, talking, singing, and playing help the brain get "wired" for future learning. And now is the time. Research shows that young babies need a lot of stimulation now so they can learn later.

Even very young babies need to play. The best thing a young baby can have to play with is her parents or another family member. Babies like to look at and touch things and to listen to things that make noise. Almost anything parents can do can seem like play to their baby. Making funny faces, saying the same sound over and over, or letting their baby see herself in a mirror are all ways to play.

As a baby gets older, she needs objects to touch, taste, hold, bang, move, and drop. But, her family is still important, too. An older baby will enjoy a game of "peek-a-boo" with someone they love.

You can encourage parents to spend time and play with their baby. You can help them feel confident playing with their baby. Tell parents when they are doing a good job and give them new ideas to try. Remind them often that playing with their baby is crucial to their baby's brain development. Encourage parents to play with their baby every day and in different ways.

Concerns to Be Aware of During Home Visits

If you notice any of these things, discuss them with the parents and/or your supervisor. Your supervisor will help you decide what needs to be done.

- Parents who do not hold their baby when feeding.
- Parents who seem scared or look very uncomfortable when they are feeding their baby.

- Parents who cannot tell when their baby is hungry or full.
- Parents who use food to comfort their baby's cries, even when their baby is not hungry.
- Parents who don't seem to feed their baby enough.
- A baby who doesn't look healthy.
- A baby who doesn't seem to be gaining weight.
- A baby who seems to be spitting up too much.
- A baby who seems to be hungry all the time even though they are being fed six to eight times each day.
- A breastfeeding mother who is having a lot of problems with her breasts.
- A parent or a baby who doesn't seem to enjoy breastfeeding.
- Parents who have trouble taking good care of their own health.
- A baby who doesn't seem to be getting milk from the bottle. For example, maybe the nipple hole is clogged or closed.
- A baby who is drinking from dirty or sour baby bottles.
- Parents who give their baby other food (like baby food or mashed up adult food) when the baby is less than six months old.
- A baby who doesn't have six to ten wet diapers each day.
- Parents who don't seem to change their baby's diapers enough.
- Parents who may not have enough money to buy enough diapers for their baby.
- Parents who seem to have a lot of trouble diapering their baby.
- A baby who seems to have diaper rash all of the time.
- A baby who looks or smells like he needs a bath each time you see him.
- Parents who don't seem to care if their baby is clean.
- Parents who don't keep themselves clean.

- Parents who don't seem concerned about their baby's safety. For example, they may talk about leaving their baby alone in or near water or talk about using very hot water for a bath.

- Parents who are having a hard time helping their baby get used to taking a bath.

- Parents who don't comfort their baby when he cries.

- Parents who get mad when their baby cries.

- A baby who never seems to cry but also never shows any other kinds of feelings (happy, bored, scared).

- Parents who always seem tired.

- Parents who don't smile or seem angry all the time.

- Parents who have very quick tempers.

- Parents who talk about being very mad at their baby.

- Parents who think that their baby is being bad by crying or is crying on purpose to make them upset.

- A baby who has bruises anywhere on his body—on his face, head, arms, or legs.

- Parents who don't watch their baby carefully during a visit.

- A baby who seems to have a lot of accidents.

- Parents who leave their baby in dangerous situations. For example, on the floor near uncovered electrical outlets or on a table or chair where the baby could fall off.

- A baby who doesn't seem happy, curious, or interested in what is happening around him.

- Parents who don't seem interested in whether their baby is growing and developing normally.

- Parents who never really watch what their baby is doing.

- Parents who never play with their baby.

- Parents who want to play with their baby, but aren't sure what to do.

- Parents who play too rough with their baby.

Feeding Your Baby:
The First Five Months

When Baby Wants to Eat: Getting Started

Getting Ready

Agenda

- **Opening:** thinking about hunger
- **Keeping It Going:** babies' signs of hunger, feeding a baby, holding a baby while feeding
- **Closing:** using what we've learned

Objectives

Parents will

- know when their baby is hungry
- understand why they should hold their baby when feeding
- know the importance of burping their baby and how to do it
- know when their baby is full

In Advance

- Review the information in the parenting information book *Baby Is Here!*
- Collect brochures from organizations such as the LaLeche League or a lactation clinic that offers support for parents who are breastfeeding.

Materials

Activity 1: Feeding Your Baby

- Young Family Parenting Information book *Baby Is Here!* for parents

Getting Ready (continued)

Activity 2: Feeding Your Baby

- newborn-size doll with head and arms that move
- selection of bottles and nipples
- A "burp cloth." This protects parents' clothes from any milk baby may spit up. It can be a clean cloth diaper, a clean dish towel, or a rubberized flannel cloth sold as a burp cloth.

When Baby Wants to Eat: Getting Started

Opening

Ask parents how they know when their baby is hungry. Review the physical clues their baby gives when she is hungry. Have the parents noticed these things with their baby? What does their baby do when she is hungry?

Keeping It Going

Activity 1: Feeding Your Baby

Go over with the parents the pages on feeding a baby in the parent information book *Baby Is Here!*.

Remind the parents that feeding time is for more than simply providing food. It is a special time between parents and their baby. When the parents hold their baby close for feeding, special physical and emotional ties grow. These ties are important for both the parents and their baby.

Ask the parents how they know when their baby has had enough to eat? Remind them to watch for the clues their baby gives when he's finished eating.

Activity 2: Feeding Your Baby

Use the doll to demonstrate the steps for feeding.
Talk about where to feed. Ask the parents where in their home they think there's a good spot for feeding their baby. A comfortable chair in a warm spot might be good. Emphasize holding the baby gently, not rushing, and feeling relaxed about the feeding.

Talk to the doll in a soft, gentle voice or sing softly as you demonstrate feeding.
Show the parents how to burp the baby.

Many experts do not encourage establishing a set "feeding schedule" of every so many hours. Encourage parents to talk about this with their health care provider.

Remind parents that not all of their baby's cries are cries of hunger.
If a baby cries soon after feeding, talk about what else might make him unhappy. Does he need to burp or have a diaper changed? Brainstorm ways to comfort their baby.

Demonstrate swaddling and other comforting techniques for a crying baby.

Talk about feeding schedules.
Ask the mom what kind of advice she has gotten about when to feed their baby. Has the dad gotten advice that is the same or different? The clinic will give parents some guidelines, but probably everyone else they know will have an opinion, too, including mothers, grandfathers, and next-door neighbors.

Parents will be able to determine their baby's feeding pattern. Use the chart in the parenting information book as an example of one baby's feeding pattern, but remind them that their baby will have his own needs and pattern. Affirm parents that they know their baby best.

Discuss any concerns the parents have about feeding.
Reassure parents that any feeding issues are usually temporary. Remind them that as their baby grows, her feeding needs and schedule change. For now, parents need to be able to recognize when their baby is hungry and to feed him then.

Closing

Help parents summarize what they learned by going over these points. You may want to add others if you notice parents need more information.

- ✓ Getting to know their baby's clues about when he is hungry or full will help parents feel confident when feeding their baby.
- ✓ Helping a baby establish a feeding routine takes time. The routine will change as the baby grows and changes.
- ✓ Feeding time is an important time for parents and their baby to grow closer.

Breastfeeding and Problems with Breastfeeding

Getting Ready

Agenda

- **Opening:** moms need support for successful breastfeeding
- **Keeping It Going:** advantages of breastfeeding and how to breastfeed
- **Closing:** using what we've learned

Objectives

Parents will

- know how a mother can take care of herself if she is breastfeeding
- know how to breastfeed
- understand the issues that surround breastfeeding

In Advance

- Review the information in the parenting information book *Baby Is Here!*

Materials

Activity I: Breastfeeding

- Young Family Parenting Information book *Baby Is Here!* for parents
- fresh celery stalk and food coloring
- supplies for healthy snacks and drinks
- copies of recipes for the snacks and drinks
- At the beginning of the visit, put one teaspoon of food coloring in 1/2 cup of water in a glass. Slice the bottom off of a stalk of celery and place it in the glass of colored water.

Getting Ready (continued)

Activity 2: How to Breastfeed

- breast pump, breast pads, ointment
- Cut out some magazine pictures of healthy foods and foods that could upset a baby's tummy if a breastfeeding mother eats them.

Breastfeeding and Problems with Breastfeeding

Opening

"Breastfeeding a baby offers several advantages. It is convenient, always available, affordable, and gives a baby a healthy boost, according to recent research. Mom needs to take care of herself and be sure she gets healthy food and plenty of rest. Dad is important to the success of breastfeeding because he can offer the needed support and extra care a mom needs."

Keeping It Going

Activity 1: Breastfeeding

Review the information on breastfeeding in the *Baby Is Here!* parent book and the advantages a baby has if she is breastfed.

Demonstrate how everything a mother eats is absorbed into her body and then passed on to the baby.
This shows why breastfeeding moms should avoid foods that may cause upset stomachs in some babies. Show the parents what has happened with the celery you put in the colored water. The celery needs the water and will draw it up through its "veins"—you will see the colored stripes rise on the celery stalk. This is what happens with us, too, as food is absorbed into our bodies.

Continue by reminding the parents that mom needs to take care of herself so she can breastfeed her baby. A balanced diet and plenty of liquids are important. Moms are often too tired from the delivery and the new responsibilities of parenting to spend much time preparing foods. You may want to go to the kitchen and help parents make some quick nutritious snacks and drinks that can help mom eat healthy foods. You may need to bring some examples of healthy snacks.

Here are some ideas:

- Fruit juice spritzer: Mix favorite fruit juice—for example, apple, cranberry, or grape —with low sodium carbonated water.

All communities have nutrition help for babies and moms. Explain the program to the parents and and how they can apply. These programs can help with purchasing formula and other healthy foods.

- Spread peanut butter on a piece of celery or apple and dot with raisins.
- Make a quick dip for fresh vegetables by mixing spices like dill or parsley in cottage cheese or low-fat sour cream or yogurt.
- Spread low fat cream cheese on a toasted bagel or a tortilla.
- String cheese is an easy, nutritious snack.

Ask what else a breastfeeding mom needs to stay healthy for her baby. Here are some ideas:

- get a lot of rest
- avoid some medications (mom should ask her health care provider before taking any medications)
- take time for herself
- help from dad or other family members

Ask the parents if mom is having trouble doing any of these things. Discuss why she may be having trouble.

Brainstorm all the ways that mom can take care of herself and ways others can help so the parents can take care of their baby.

Ask:

- Is there anywhere else a parent can get support for breastfeeding? (The baby's clinic, the lactation consultant at the hospital, or their health care provider.)

Activity 2: How to Breastfeed
Talk about how to breastfeed.
Discuss any questions the parents may have about breastfeeding. Is mom having problems with engorgement, sore nipples, or anything else? Discuss some ways to make the mother more comfortable.

Demonstrate the breast pump and talk about when it might be used.
For example, breast milk can be put into a bottle for dad or others to feed the baby. Discuss where to get a breast pump if it's needed.

Remind parents that dad can participate in breastfeeding, too. He may give the baby a bottle of breast milk that mom expressed. He can get the baby in the night and bring him to mom for feeding. He can burp the baby when the baby is done eating.

Review "Taking Care of Breasts" in the parenting information book.

Show parents breast pads and ointments and explain their use.

Discuss any concerns parents may have about feeding their baby, including what, when, and is it enough?

Discuss how parents feel about breastfeeding in public.

Parents may be concerned about the reaction of others if they choose to breastfeed in public areas or away from home.

Brainstorm ideas to deal with these issues.

Demonstrate some ideas such as using a small blanket to drape from mom's shoulder over the baby when breastfeeding. Talk about different types of shirts, tops, and bras that make breastfeeding easier.

Practice some responses for parents to try if people are critical of breastfeeding or try to discourage it.

Fathers can make a big difference in how successful a mom is with breastfeeding. He can respond to critics in his own way and offer his support to mom.

Closing

Help parents summarize what they learned by going over these points. You may want to add others if you notice parents need more information.

- ✓ Breastfeeding can be a healthy and convenient choice for feeding a baby.
- ✓ A breastfeeding mom needs to take care of herself by eating well, getting enough rest, and avoiding foods and medications that could affect her baby.
- ✓ Dad and other family members can help mom by supporting her choice to breastfeed and by helping making her comfortable, giving her help when she needs it, and more.

Bottle-feeding and Problems with Bottle-feeding

Agenda

- **Opening:** thinking about bottle-feeding
- **Keeping It Going:** all about formula; preparing to bottle-fed
- **Closing:** using what we've learned

Objectives

Parents will

- be able to decide between breast or bottle-feeding or a combination
- understand the different types of baby formula and which type is best for their baby

In Advance

- Review the information in the parenting information book *Baby Is Here!*

Materials

Activity 1: Bottle-feeding

- Young Family Parenting Information book *Baby Is Here!* for parents
- newborn-size doll (optional unless parent is still pregnant)
- A variety of types and brands of formula, including soy, formula for older babies, and iron-enriched formula. Include powdered, concentrated, and ready-to-feed formulas. You can use empty cans as long as they have the labels on them. Have one full can of each type on hand.
- a variety of nipples and bottles
- mixing and measuring spoons and cups
- water source

Getting Ready (continued)

Activity 2: Bottle-feeding

- a list of prices for various kinds of formula at different stores listed on a chart

Bottle-feeding and Problems with Bottle-feeding

Opening

"Bottlefeeding will give your baby the nutrition she needs, but parents need to know about the various kinds of formula, bottles, and nipples so they can choose what works best for their baby."

Keeping It Going

Activity 1: Bottle-feeding

Go over the bottle-feeding section in the parenting information book.
Ask parents to show you how they bottle-feed their baby, if they are comfortable with that. Otherwise demonstrate using the doll. Talk about how the parent is holding the baby close and make other positive comments. You can show how to hold the baby close, how to burp, and how to talk to the baby.

Continue by discussing the various types of nipples and bottles. Ask the parents if they have other kinds. Most are fine; remind parents to be sure that the nipples don't have tears or holes that are too big. The brand or type to use is the one baby seems to like best.

Remind parents that moms who bottle-feed their babies need to take care of themselves and eat right, too.
You can use the ideas in the previous topic for healthy snacks and other ways for mom to take care of herself.

Point out the pros and cons of each type of formula as discussed in the parenting information book.
Each brand of formula is fine for baby. Which of these the parents choose to use depends on availability and personal circumstances. Remind parents to ask their health care providers if there is a special kind of formula (for example: soy, low iron, or iron fortified) their baby needs.

Demonstrate how to mix different kinds of formula.
The most important thing to get across is to mix the formula according to directions. Do not add more water than is called for. Discuss this

All communities have nutrition help for babies and moms. Explain the program to the parents and and how they can apply. These programs can help with purchasing formula and other healthy foods.

with the parents. Be sure to talk about buying formula in reputable stores, looking for signs of tampering, and following the directions.

Demonstrate how to wash and dry nursing bottles and nipples.
Clean bottles and nipples are important for baby's health.

Activity 2: How to Bottle-feed

Formula comes in different strengths and styles. The most convenient is *ready-to-feed,* where parents open the can and pour it in the bottle or, just put a nipple on the bottle. Another form is a *liquid concentrate,* where parents add water to before feeding. The third type is *powdered,* where parents measure the powder into a bottle or other clean container, add water, and mix. Each type has advantages, but there can be big cost differences among the types.

Show parents the chart you made. Discuss the differences in price and convenience of each type of formula. Ask the parents where they buy their formula. Do they look for price or convenience first? What have they decided?

End the visit by discussing any concerns the parents may have about feeding their baby including what, when, and is it enough?
Questions like these are answered in the parenting information book *Baby Is Here!*

Closing

Help parents summarize what they learned by going over these points. You may want to add others if you notice parents need more information.

✓ Bottle-feeding with formula will give a baby the nutrition she needs.

✓ To be sure their baby is getting the proper nutrition from formula, parents must follow all the directions for mixing formula.

✓ Keeping bottles and nipples clean is important for the health of the baby.

✓ Convenience and price varies among different types of formula.

Keeping Your Baby Clean

Diapers

Agenda

- **Opening:** different types of diapers
- **Keeping It Going:** choosing diapers and how to diaper
- **Closing:** using what we've learned

Objectives

Parents will

- decide what type of diaper (disposable or cloth) works best for their baby and for them
- learn how to diaper a baby

In Advance

- Review the information in the parenting information book *Baby Is Here!*

Materials

Activity 1: Which Diaper?

- Young Family Parenting Information book *Baby Is Here!* for parents.
- Cloth diapers from store and diaper service.
- Several different brands and types of disposable diapers. Try to have national and store brands and a variety of types: boy or girl, overnight, ultra absorbent, etc. Sharing the newest thing in disposable diapers would be good, too.
- Information on costs of disposable diapers at different stores. Check on national brands like Huggies and Pampers and store brands.
- Gather some coupons for different brands of disposable diapers.
- Get similar cost information for cloth diapers at Kids 'R' Us, J. C. Penney, Target, or other stores.

Getting Ready (continued)

- Get information on the cost of laundry soap for diapers and bleach.
- Information on diaper services for cloth diapers (if available).
- Make a chart showing the various costs. Look in the parenting information for a sample chart; it shows what to include.
- calculator
- paper and pencil for recording diaper cost calculations

Activity 2: Are Diapers Different?
- 1-cup measuring cup
- water source
- cloth diapers from a store and diaper service
- Several different brands and types of disposable diapers. Try to have national brands and store brands and a variety of types: boy or girl, overnight, ultra absorbent, etc. Whatever is the newest thing in disposables would be good, too.

Activity 3: How to Diaper Your Baby
- diapers from the above activities
- newborn-size doll
- alcohol-free baby wipes
- diaper rash ointment
- diaper pins for cloth diapers
- plastic pants
- diaper bag, backpack, or other bag to use as a diaper bag

Diapers

Opening

"If you go to a department store or grocery store, you will see dozens of sizes and brands of diapers. Then, if you look at cloth diapers or a diaper service that delivers clean diapers and picks up the soiled ones, you have even more choices. How do you know which one works best at the best price? This chart helps us see how costs compare."

Keeping It Going

Activity 1: Which Diaper?

Show the parents the various kinds of diapers—disposable and cloth.
Talk about the kind of diapers the parents are using. Why did they choose that type?

Discuss the different costs and issues associated with using each type of diaper. Look at the chart in *Baby Is Here!* parent book for the items needed with different types of diapers.
Use the chart comparing the prices of different types of diapers using the information you have from local diaper services and the ads for disposable diapers. Calculate the cost per diaper (divide the price of the package or service by the number of diapers in the package or weekly delivery). Then discuss the pros and cons of the different types, including:

- washing your own diapers (access to a washing machine and dryer, soap to wash diapers, container to keep soiled diapers in)

- fit may differ among the types of diapers

- place to leave dirty and clean diapers for a diaper service

- easy to use away from home

- getting bulky packs of disposable diapers home from store

Ask what other considerations there might be for using either type of diaper.

Activity 2: Are Diapers Different?

Another thing to look at is how well the diapers work. How well do the diapers hold water?

Place the disposable diapers and a cloth diaper on a table or counter top along with the pitcher of water and measuring cup. Ask the parents to pour about 1/4 cup of water on each diaper.

When the diapers are wet, ask the parents to look at each diaper and think about these questions:

- What do you notice about the diapers when they are wet?

- How does the cloth diaper feel?

- How do each of the disposable diapers feel?

- Does one of the disposables have a liner? Does that make it feel dryer than the cloth diaper?

- How well does each kind of diaper hold the water?

- Do you think your baby will notice the difference between different kinds of diapers?

Continue by asking the parents to decide which of the diapers seems to hold the most water. Is that the best diaper?

Discuss other features of the diapers, especially the disposable ones, to see what other factors might make a difference in the choice. Look at the tabs, the elastic, the weight of the plastic, the feel of the material, etc.

Based on this discussion, ask the parents what they think about the different types of diapers.

Remind them that they can use different types of diapers at different times. For example, use cloth diapers at home and disposable ones when away from home. Affirm the parents' choice of the one best for their family.

Point out to the parents that newborns use about ten diapers a day, making diaper changes a big part of the day for both parents and their baby.

Activity 3: How to Diaper Your Baby

Demonstrate how to diaper a baby using the doll and the different types of diapers.
Ask the parents which diaper seems easier and faster to use. If parents agree, you can help diaper the real baby, too. This may be the real challenge, since the doll doesn't wriggle around or cry!

Let parents practice diapering.
Wriggly babies can be hard to change. Brainstorm ways to keep the baby interested and still during a diaper change.

Talk about the causes of diaper rash.
Diaper rash makes a baby's bottom hurt. It is caused by being in a wet diaper too long, sensitivity to the type of disposable diaper, a reaction to the soap that cloth diapers are washed in, or an allergy to certain foods.

Talk about what to do about diaper rash.
Remind parents that they will need to be ready to change a diaper wherever they take their baby. Acknowledge that taking a baby on an outing can sometimes seem overwhelming because babies seem to need a lot of things. It is easier for parents if they keep a diaper bag packed and ready to go.

There are many different sizes and types of diaper bags. Parents may also use a tote bag or carrier bag. Discuss what might work best for them. Talk about alternatives to diaper bags that parent may already have (a backpack or athletic bag, for example).

Brainstorm a list of things to include in a diaper bag. Here are some ideas:

- extra diapers
- change of clothes
- baby wipes
- pacifier
- small toy
- blanket or pad to lay baby on to change
- washcloth

Comment on how well the parents are doing when they are changing and dressing their baby. Point out how much they already know.

- bottle and powdered formula (if using formula)
- phone numbers you may need
- rash ointment

You may want to talk about responsibly discarding disposal diapers. They should never be flushed down the toilet. They should be wrapped up in newspaper or a plastic bag and put in the trash. In public places, don't leave used diapers anywhere but in a trash can.

Remind parents to dispose of used diapers in the appropriate manner. They can save plastic bags, like bread bags, to carry home soiled cloth diapers. Throw disposable diapers away in a trash container in a restroom or other spot.

Closing

Help parents summarize what they learned by going over these points. You may want to add others if you notice parents need more information.

✓ There is a wide variety of diapers from which parents may choose. Parents can look at the pros and cons of each type and choose the best one for their baby and family.

✓ Babies are happier and healthier when they are clean and dry.

✓ Parents can help their baby feel more comfortable during their daily routine of diapering.

✓ Daily routines such as diapering provide a chance for parents to talk to and touch their baby, showing her how much they love her.

Baths

Agenda

- **Opening:** worries about bathing a baby
- **Keeping It Going:** learning to bathe a baby
- **Closing:** using what we've learned

Objectives

Parents will

- understand the importance of keeping their baby clean and dry
- practice giving their baby a bath
- learn how to keep bathtime safe
- learn how to keep their baby clean between baths
- understand that bathing their baby gives parents a chance to play with him

In Advance

- Review the information in the parenting information book *Baby Is Here!*
- Check with parents to be sure it is okay to bathe their baby while you are there. If not, take a doll you can use to demonstrate.
- Ask parents where they bathe their baby—baby tub, kitchen sink, bathtub. Ask if there is anything you can think of that might make bathing their babies easier.

Materials

Activity 1: Giving Your Baby a Bath

- Young Family Parenting Information book *Baby Is Here!* for parents
- doll (optional, see above)
- mild soap, washcloth, towels
- cotton ball and rubbing alcohol if umbilical cord is still attached

Baths

Opening

"Acknowledge that many new parents worry about giving their baby a bath. Wet babies are slippery and squirmy. Parents may worry about dropping their babies. Babies may cry or fuss about being in the tub. Keeping a baby safe is the most important part of bathing."

Keeping It Going

Activity 1: Giving Your Baby a Bath

Talk with the parents about their worries or concerns when bathing their baby. You can ask questions like these:

- Have the parents had any problems bathing their baby?

- Does their baby like baths? Does the baby's enjoyment or fear of baths make it easier or harder to bathe their baby? How?

Go over the steps for both sponge and tub baths in the parenting information book.
Demonstrate each step of both types of bath using the doll. Be sure to talk to the "baby" while you're bathing him. If parents want, have them give their baby a bath. Help the parents find a good spot—bathtub, kitchen sink—that is warm and safe for their baby. Have all the supplies at hand. Try turning on soft music to help calm the baby.

Talk about any safety devices parents may have seen for giving a baby a bath, such as a ring with suction cups that helps keep the baby upright in the tub or a large sponge that is shaped like a tub to keep the baby from slipping.
These items may help the parents handle their child in the bath, but they are no substitute for the parents being there every minute. Under no circumstances should a baby or child be left alone in the bathtub, not even for a few seconds. Remind parents to let the phone or doorbell ring or to take baby with them.

Be sure to emphasize safety in the bathtub. A baby can drown in very little water.

Talk about ways to make bathtime fun.
With their baby in the bath, encourage the parents to play with their baby by dribbling a stream of water on his tummy, tickling his toes, or showing him some bath toys. Both baby and parents can enjoy baby's baths.

Point out other bathroom safety rules.

- Keep any and all electric appliances (hair dryers, curling irons, razors, radios, and other electrical equipment) away from the bath area. A baby could pull one into water and be electrocuted.

- Keep objects away from the bath area that baby could pull into the water or onto herself. This includes heavy shampoo bottles, baskets of supplies, or towels.

- Test the water before putting the baby into it. Test it by putting your elbow in the water; it should be about body temperature, so parents shouldn't feel hot or cold sensations when touching the water.

- Always hold onto the baby when she's in the water.

Ask what other safety concerns parents might have about bathing their baby.
Discuss these concerns and help the parents find ways to address or lessen these safety concerns.

Closing

Help parents summarize what they learned by going over these points. You may want to add others if you notice parents need more information.

- ✓ Parents can learn how to safely give their baby a bath.
- ✓ Baths can be enjoyable for both the baby and her parents with some preparation and play.
- ✓ Babies can be kept clean with a combination of tub and sponge baths.
- ✓ **Never** leave a baby alone in or near the water.

Help for a Crying Baby

Baby Cries

Agenda
- **Opening:** why babies cry
- **Keeping It Going:** comforting a crying baby (and ourselves)
- **Closing:** using what we've learned

Objectives
Parents will

- understand why babies cry
- learn ways to soothe a crying baby
- learn ways to deal with their own feelings when their baby cries

In Advance
- Review the information in the parenting information book *Baby Is Here!*

Materials

Activity 1: Why Babies Cry
- Young Family Parenting Information book *Baby Is Here!* for parents
- Make cards with the different reasons a baby might cry. *Baby Is Here!* lists some of the reasons. You can add others.

Activity 2: Comforting Your Baby
- Young Family Parenting Information book *Baby Is Here!* for parents
- baby blanket
- pacifier
- other comfort objects for a baby

Getting Ready (continued)

Activity 3: What Parents Feel

- Young Family Parenting Information book *Baby Is Here!* for parents

- Make a tape recording of different babies' cries.

- A tape player/recorder to record the cry of the baby who lives here. (It's possible, of course, the baby may not cry!)

Baby Cries

Opening _____

"There are many reasons babies cry. They may be hungry, tired, cold, or just need to let off steam."

Keeping It Going_____

Activity 1: Why Babies Cry

Place the cards face down on a table.
Have the parents choose a card and ask the question, "How does a baby tell you she needs this?" Continue with the other cards. The answer to all the questions is, "She cries!"

Challenge the parents to figure out which cry means what.
Play the different babies' cries and try to guess what the baby is saying. There are no right answers to this. The idea is to just listen to the different sounds babies make when they cry.

If possible, record a cry of the baby who lives here.
Then play the cry back amid the cries of the other babies. Can the parents pick out their baby's cry? Why was the baby crying this time?

Review the information in the parenting information book about why babies cry.

Activity 2: Comforting Your Baby

Ask the parents if they have found ways to comfort their crying baby. Is there something that works best when their baby is tired?

Brainstorm different ways to comfort a crying baby. Here are some ways to comfort a baby:

- swaddling the baby (wrapping her tightly in a blanket)
- rocking or walking
- rubbing the baby's back
- offering the baby a pacifier or helping the baby suck her thumb

You or the parents can demonstrate these different methods.

Activity 3: What Parents Feel

Play the tape of the crying baby.
Let it play for awhile and encourage the parents to imagine that it is their baby. Talk about how listening to the cry makes parents feel. Talk about their baby. Has their baby ever cried like that? Could they figure out why their baby was crying? How did they help their baby?

Talk about how parents might feel when their baby cries and cries and just can't seem to be comforted. It can be very frustrating. Parents may feel worried, angry, tired, insecure, scared, or sad.

What can the parents do? Talk about the ideas in their parenting information book. Would any of the suggestions work for them?

Practice some of the soothing techniques you discussed above.

Review the *Baby Is Here!* information on how parents might feel when their baby cries.

Talk about what not to do, too. There is important information in the parenting information book.

Here are some things parents should **never** do when their baby cries and cries:

- NEVER SHAKE THE BABY. This can cause brain damage and seriously harm their baby's body.
- Never leave the baby alone in house or apartment while they go cool off.
- Don't cover the baby's head with a blanket or pillow.
- Don't hit the baby.
- Don't shout at the baby.

If you think the parents need help in findings ways to cool off, brainstorm some ideas. Here are some things they can consider:

- Have a "parent" time out. Go into another room until you are calm.
- Stop where you are. Step back. Sit down.
- Take 5 deep breaths. Inhale. Exhale.
- Count to 10 or even count to 20.
- Say the alphabet out loud.

- Call a relative or friend.
- Hug a pillow.
- Chew on an apple.
- Do some exercises.
- Take a hot bath or a cold shower.
- Lie down on the floor, or just put your feet up.
- Listen to your favorite music.
- Call a crisis nursery or help line in your community.

Remind the parents that if they try any method that takes them away from their baby—a time out or a bath, for example—they need to be sure their baby is in a safe place first.

Closing

Help parents summarize what they learned by going over these points. You may want to add others if you notice parents need more information.

- ✓ Babies cry for different reasons at different ages.
- ✓ When parents respond to their baby's cries, the baby knows that what he needs is important to them. Responding to his needs lets him know he is loved.
- ✓ Babies cannot be spoiled by being comforted when they cry.
- ✓ Parents can learn different ways to soothe their crying baby.
- ✓ All parents feel helpless and frustrated when faced with a crying baby. It is important to try to help the baby, but it is also important to take time to cool ourselves off.

Keeping Your Baby Safe

Twenty Rules to Keep Baby Safe

Agenda

- **Opening:** what accidents can happen to babies
- **Keeping It Going:** learning to keep your baby safe
- **Closing:** using what we've learned

Objectives

Parents will

- learn 20 rules for keeping their baby safe

In Advance

- Review the information in the parenting information book *Baby Is Here!*

Materials

Activity 1: 20 Rules

- Young Family Parenting Information book *Baby Is Here!* for parents
- Make cards from the pictures in the parenting information book by photocopying the pictures and pasting them on index cards or heavy paper.
- Mark each card with the rule number it shows.
- basic childproofing supplies like outlet covers and cupboard locks

Twenty Rules to Keep Baby Safe

Opening

"Without rules, life would be very confusing and disorganized. Rules help keep people safe. Parents need to know some safety rules to help keep their baby safe."

Keeping It Going

Activity 1: 20 Rules

Briefly introduce the safety game.
Explain that the cards show ways to keep baby safe and things that might hurt baby. Point out that their Young Family Parenting Information book lists these 20 rules for keeping their baby safe.

Begin by turning over each card and talking about what it shows. For the first go round, keep the cards in order by rule.

Mix up the cards.
Ask the parents to look at each card and discuss the safety rule or danger each represents. Encourage discussion about safety and ways parents can keep their baby safe by following rules like these, looking at each situation with safety in mind, and always being careful.

Look at safety from a baby's view.
Ask the parents to join you in getting down on their hands and knees to look for possible safety hazards from a new angle. Discuss with parents ways to fix any that are discovered.

Now ask the parents to look around their home and identify things that might be unsafe for their baby.
Are there houseplants the baby might reach? An uncovered electrical outlet? Small items on the floor?

Recognize any safety precautions parents may already have in place.
Congratulate them on the good care they give to their baby by keeping him safe.

These safety rules are presented for babies. As a baby grows, it will be important to reconsider these rules and expand childproofing efforts. More information about childproofing can be found in the parent book *Safe Child and Emergencies*.

Show parents where to find the rules in the parenting information book so they can refer back to them as they work to keep their baby safe.

Parents may want to talk about accidents they have had with their baby or accidents they have heard about.
As part of this conversation, talk about ways the accident could have been prevented.

Show the parents the safety and childproofing equipment.
Help the parents understand how to use and install the equipment. Share information about costs and where they can purchase or obtain them for free. Remind the parents that it is up to them to keep their baby safe. They can do this by making sure dangerous things like small objects and medicines are kept away from their baby and the house is made safe by blocking the stairs, covering outlets, etc. Parents will need to do more and different childproofing as their baby grows.

Closing

Help parents summarize what they learned by going over these points. You may want to add others if you notice parents need more information.

- ✓ Keeping their baby safe is an important part of being a parent.
- ✓ Childproofing the home should be done as soon as a baby can begin to grab things and move around.
- ✓ Following safety rules and keeping their baby safe in other ways takes a lot of time, but it is very important. Parents should be proud of how well they take care of their baby.

Having Fun with Your Baby

Getting to Know Your Baby

Agenda

- **Opening:** getting to know your baby
- **Keeping It Going:** how to learn about your baby
- **Closing:** using what we've learned

Objectives

Parents will

- begin to understand their baby
- learn ways to play with their baby

In Advance

- Review the information in the parenting information book *Baby Is Here!*

Materials

Activity 1: Getting to Know Your Baby

- Young Family Parenting Information book *Baby Is Here!* for parents
- plain paper and crayons or markers

Activity 2: Little Things Mean a Lot

- Young Family Parenting Information book *Baby Is Here!* for parents
- baby toys
- copy of the Little Things Mean a Lot handout from the back of this section

Getting to Know Your Baby

Opening

"Getting to know your baby is important because it can help you help your baby grow. You will have a better understanding of what your baby likes and doesn't like and what makes her feel safe and secure. By making everyday activities nurturing times with your baby, you are building a long-lasting, loving relationship with her."

Keeping It Going

Activity 1: Getting to Know Your Baby

Ask parents to describe how their baby acts when he is happy, sad, sick, hungry, angry, etc.

Remind parents that getting to know their baby is good so they can help their baby grow the best he can.

Point out that getting to know their baby is one of the truly enjoyable aspects of parenting.

Encourage the parents to take time to stand back and watch their baby. This is a time to wonder who this little person is and dream of what he will become.

Sit on the floor with the parents and their baby.

As you watch the their baby, point out all the things their baby is doing. Talk about their baby's personality and temperament, how she moves, ways she responds to different things, what she seems to like and dislike, and other things you and the parents learn from watching her.

Give parents the paper and crayons or markers.

Ask the parents to draw a picture of some of the things they know about their baby. Begin by drawing their baby in the center of the page. Then around it put pictures, words, or symbols describing their baby. Use the questions in the parenting information book to give the parents some ideas. For example, if their baby likes to hear sounds, the parent can draw musical notes or sound symbols. An active baby could be pictured waving her arms and legs. Suggest that parents date the picture and put it in a place where it can be seen and kept safe.

This is a great activity to show parents how to get one-on-one and face-to-face with their baby. You have the opportunity to demonstrate activities and play that will help parents get to know their baby better. Help parents individualize the interaction to suit their unique way of relating to their child.

Ask parents how they can use the information they have learned from watching their baby.
Continue the discussion by asking why it matters that parents take time to get to know their baby.

Here are some ideas:

- Parents will know what upsets their baby and can avoid such situations.

- It might be easier to entertain their baby if they know what their baby likes.

- By responding to their baby's cues, parents will build trust between them and their baby.

Point out that by playing with and learning about their baby, parents are developing an attachment to him and he to them.
This is an important foundation for their relationship as their baby grows.

Activity 2: Little Things Mean a Lot

Ask the parents if they have noticed things other people (grandparents, relatives, friends) do when they are holding, changing, or feeding their baby.
Talk about what their baby seems to like and what she doesn't seem to like. Have the parents learned anything from watching others with their baby? What?

Now ask the parents to sit on the floor facing their baby. Allow a few minutes for them to talk and play with their baby. Note something positive about each interaction between the parents and their baby.

Watch for

- talking, cooing, gurgling

- peek-a-boo, other games

- eye contact, touching hands

- toy play

- mimicking each other

Affirm parents for the positive interaction.
Comment on how natural it is for parents to nurture their babies.

Continue by asking parents to place their baby on a blanket on the floor.
Point out that caring for their baby by feeding, bathing, diapering, and playing are some of the most important things parents do. Tell parents that these times with their baby are a good time to get to know their baby and to stimulate learning. Point out that they don't need anything other than their voices, their touch, and their faces.

With the baby on the blanket, show the parents how to make eye contact with their baby, speak quietly, and touch her gently.

Ask the parents to show their baby a toy. Encourage them to talk to her and make remarks like, "You are a wonderful baby!" or "How smart you are!" Point out how the baby responds to the parent's voice.

Keep going by asking how the parents encourage and communicate with their baby while they do everyday things like diapering.
Have they found different things their baby likes, such as a favorite toy to hold while diapering? Ask the parents what songs or games they sing and play with their baby.

Ask the parents to continue interacting with their baby. Discuss how everyday tasks can turn into fun times with their baby.

- Touching and talking during feeding time.
- Singing to their baby at bathtime.
- Rocking and cuddling their baby at bathtime.
- Gently touching and talking to their baby during diapering.

Encourage the parents to do this nurturing with their baby whenever doing everyday tasks.

Give the parents a copy of the Little Things Mean a Lot handout at the end of this section as a reminder of things they can do with their baby.

Many parents appreciate and learn from having the home visitor photograph or videotape them playing with and caring for their child. Let the family keep this special record as a gift.

Closing

Help parents summarize what they learned by going over these points. You may want to add others if you notice parents need more information.

- ✓ Parents who get to know their baby will be able to respond better to their baby's moods and needs.
- ✓ Closely watching their baby is a good way to learn what an unusual and unique person their baby is.

Baby Plays

Agenda

- **Opening:** how does a baby play
- **Keeping It Going:** ways to play with your baby
- **Closing:** using what we've learned

Objectives

Parents will

- learn how to play with their infants and young children

In Advance

- Review the information in the parenting information book *Baby Is Here!*

Materials

Activity 1: Playing with Your Baby

- safe, colorful toys for the baby to look at and hold
- unbreakable mirror
- plain paper and markers or crayons
- radio, CD or tape player, ticking clock, musical instruments, music box, or toys that make sounds
- copy of the Baby Thoughts handout from the back of this section

Baby Plays

Opening

"Some parents may think that infants are not aware enough to play or that babies don't need to play. Research now shows that playing with babies, even the youngest ones, is important in helping their brains and muscles develop. It is important in developing the ties that grow between parents and child, too. But how do parents play with an infant or young baby?"

Keeping It Going

Activity 1: Playing with Your Baby

Toys are one way to play with a baby. Show the parents the toys you brought.

Ask the parents to hold their baby so they have a good view of their baby's face. Ask one parent to begin talking to the baby with their face about a foot away from the baby's face. Then ask them, slowly move their face from one side to the other as they continue to talk.

Ask parents to comment on what their baby does.

- Does the baby look at their face? Does he follow their face with his head or eyes?
- Does their baby become quiet and watchful?

Continue by asking the parents to start a conversation with their baby. It can be anything or just words said in a soft, conversational tone. What does their baby do? Does she "talk" back?

Have the parents take turns holding a plaything in front of their baby's face. Move it slowly to each side of their baby's head and then up and down. What does their baby do?

Remind parents that babies find household objects just as interesting as "toys."

Turn on the radio or CD or tape player with quiet music.

Ask parents to watch what their baby does. Does their baby like the music? How can they tell? Next, ask the parents to make some noises using the musical instruments or by singing, whistling, or using a rattle or other toy that makes noise. Which sound does their baby like best?

Brainstorm some other ways to play with their baby. For example

- Have a long "conversation" with their baby. Use words to describe what the parent is doing, babble back and forth, mimic sounds their baby makes.

- Take their baby for a walk in a front pack or stroller and talk about what you see.

- Show their baby different objects. If the baby is old enough to hold things, offer him something safe and interesting to hold.

Show the parents how much babies like faces.

The baby will like the faces of siblings, too. Encourage brothers and sisters to amuse the baby by making funny faces or playing the mirror game or peek-a-boo.

Show the parents the unbreakable mirror. Have the parents and their baby look in the mirror together. How does their baby react? Give the parents paper and markers and ask them to draw bold, simple faces. Show the faces to their baby. Does their baby seem to like these faces?

Remind the parents that playing rough, even when done for fun, can hurt their baby.

Parents should **never** shake their baby, toss their baby in the air, or jump up and down with their baby. Play music and show them how to gently "dance" with their baby, holding their baby close to their body and supporting his back and neck. Or, lay the baby on her back and gently move her arms and legs in time to the music.

Now ask the parents to look around to see if they can find other ways to play with their baby by using things around their house.

Remind the parents to always keep safety first when using toys or household objects to entertain their baby.

If the parents seem interested, go over the handout Baby Thoughts. It provides some basic information about brain development in young children.

Babies don't need toys as much as they need the interaction and conversation with parents, but simple household objects can be "toys," too. Play peek-a-boo behind a dish towel or use a wooden spoon like a baton to interest the baby.

"Point out that their baby likes to play with them. Babies enjoy seeing faces and hearing music and trying new things. Play is important even for the youngest babies because it helps their brain development and strengthens ties between them and their parents."

Closing

Help parents summarize what they learned by going over these points. You may want to add others if you notice parents need more information.

- ✓ Play is important to helping babies' brains develop. It stimulates their senses and encourages development.
- ✓ Play strengthens the ties between parents and child.
- ✓ Parents should play with their baby every day in different ways. It is never a waste of time to play with their baby.

Handouts

Little Things Mean a Lot

A few basics really show your love for your baby and all you need is your face, your touch, the sound of your voice, and the gentleness exchanged between you and your baby. Here are a few little things that mean a lot.

In General

When you respond to your baby's cry you are teaching her that she is valuable, that the world can be trusted, and that language (crying) has purpose. By trying to discover why your baby is crying—is she hungry, sick, too cold or warm, scared, bored or lonely, tired or overstimulated, wet? By responding, your baby learns that she is loved.

Babies learn and grow best when they are cared for by warm, kind people who respond to their needs and give them opportunities to touch and explore the things in their world.

Keep your baby near family and friends during meals and gatherings. Listening and watching others who care about each other is a wonderful way to learn.

About Hearing

Talk, hum, sing, or whistle during bathing, changing, playtime, and feeding.

Play music for a short time, but not all the time and not too loudly. Try different kinds of music.

Sew a bell very tightly on each sock. Your baby should never be able to pull the bell off—she could choke on it.

Talk to your baby from different places in the room. Your baby will begin to put sight and sound together.

Let your baby hear things like a clock and windchime.

Give your baby your total attention and talk or babble to him in a friendly, soothing voice. Talk about what you are doing, how much you love him, how beautiful, smart, and strong he is.

Avoid very loud noises—including music and machines. A baby's hearing is delicate.

About Touching and Feeling

Try holding your baby in different positions.

Cuddle, kiss, and gently stroke her face.

Rock while holding your baby.

When on his back, gently move your baby's arms above his head or push his legs up by bending his knees.

(continued)

With your baby on her stomach, gently push against her feet with your hands.

Always avoid rough handling. NEVER shake your baby. Babies can be badly hurt or die from being shaken or tossed.

About Seeing

Move your baby to different places or positions once in awhile. Let her watch you while you are moving about in another part of the room.

Place patterned sheets and other safe things to look at on or above your baby's bed.

Move a small flashlight or toy in front of your baby.

Play peek-a-boo or make a toy disappear and reappear. Act surprised!

Hold your baby in front of a mirror or near a window. Talk about what you see.

Baby Thoughts

Your baby bats at a toy which responds with a musical wobble. **Zip!** Your toddler is learning to run with open-armed abandon. **Zap!** Your three-year-old laughs with joy at the stories you read together. **Zing!**

All parents have seen that look of amazement and wonder on their child's face. The look tells us something special is going on inside of that little head, zip!—something has been learned, zap!—a new connection made, zing! These important connections are part of a physical process called *brain development*. Brain development helps our children continue to learn. Researchers have found that the first three years of life are an important time for learning. Here are five essential things parents can do to help children learn.

Love That Baby — Attachment

When babies feel loved, safe, and in a world that is predicable, they feel free to explore and learn. Securely attached babies become more self-confident, curious, and are better able to adjust to new situations. These skills help children be open to even more learning. The regular loving care and attention you give to your little one promotes the brain development that will last a lifetime. There is nothing more important and basic to learning and development than the love you show to your child.

Wow! — Stimulation

Who does your baby rely on most for fun and excitement? You. Parents provide the most wonderful learning experiences. A safe and

stimulating environment offers experiences that help create the "wiring" in a baby's brain. Give your child your time and attention each and every day: sing, play, read books, laugh, pretend, dance, and cuddle. Look into your child's eyes and tell him how much you love him. Show your baby how to do things and, sometimes, just step back and watch your child learn and grow. If you look at your baby's face very carefully, you can almost see "brain development" happening before your eyes.

Right from the Start — Early Learning

Research has found that children have a best or optimum time to learn certain things. The first three years are when the brain is best able to develop important connections. There are optimum times to learn about language, to develop muscles, and to learn about themselves and others. There is even a "best time" to learn how to learn. If important brain development is missed in the infant and toddler years, there are ways to compensate later on. But having to compensate can make it harder to learn. Nurture your child's brain development by offering a variety of opportunities right from the start.

(continued)

Feeling Good — Healthy Baby

Babies shouldn't smoke, drink, do drugs, or eat junk food. But parents' poor nutrition, smoking, and chemical abuse impact their child's brain development even more than we once believed. Steps toward healthy development include regular health care and immunizations, good family nutrition, safe environments, drug/alcohol abuse-free family members, and violence prevention measures.

The Care and Development of the Real Expert — You!

Take advantage of information that gives you and your children a "head start" in life. Take a parent education class, join a support group, or check out books and videos from the library. Talk with other parents about your joys, concerns, and experiences. And remember, you are the expert when it comes to your child's brain development. You are needed and important—take good care of yourself.

Chapter 2
Feeding Your Child

Introduction

Home Visitor Information

Food is a big part of most families' lives. Most celebrations include food. Special foods are served on special occasions. Everyone has favorite foods and we are surrounded by food commercials. Parents may use food as rewards or bribes for their children. Sometimes parents may make a big deal about certain kinds of foods. With all this attention paid to food, it is easy to lose sight of the purpose of food—to keep us alive and give us the energy needed to do all of our daily activities. *Feeding Your Child* helps parents sort out information about food and make knowledgable decisions about feeding their child.

"Things to Know First" can be done with parents with children of any age. It is an introduction to food and its effect on our lives. This helps parents understand why they look at food the way they do.

"Ideas to Help" has information about finger foods and making baby food at home. This information is appropriate for both older babies and toddlers. You can use either or both of these activities if the baby is six months old (the age to introduce solid foods). You can share these activities if parents need ideas about finger foods or making baby food. The other sections have age-specific information.

The "Ideas to Help" section in the Young Family Parenting Information book *Feeding Your Child* has tips for how to stop breastfeeding, if parents are at that point. Review the information with parents and discuss any questions and concerns they may have.

After doing the activities in *Feeding Your Child*, parents will

- discuss the importance of food and eating to their families and children
- learn their baby's eating habits and the signals that show he is hungry or full
- understand that a healthy diet is important for their baby's growth and development
- know what foods to avoid for babies under one year old

- learn what babies eat at different ages
- learn how to introduce new foods to their baby
- understand that toddlers have different nutrition needs as they grow
- learn tips on getting a toddler to eat what he needs
- learn about finger foods for children who are old enough to eat them
- learn how to make baby food at home

Important Information for Home Visitors

- Much of what we learn and feel about food is closely tied to our family and cultural background. Parents can celebrate their heritage by feeding their families traditional foods as part of their regular meals or on special occasions.

- Parents may experience conflict or get unwanted advice from others when it comes to buying and preparing food for themselves and their young babies. Information and support helps parents make the best choices for their family.

- Eating is closely tied to our emotions. A baby and her parents may eat differently when they are stressed, happy, or sad, or at times when they are not on their normal schedule.

- For the first six months of life, most babies only need breast milk or infant formula to eat. When babies are about six months old, they can begin eating solid foods, but breast milk or formula needs to be continued until the baby is one year old. Babies should not have cow's milk until after one year of age.

- Parents should watch their baby when offering new foods to make sure the baby doesn't have any food sensitivities.

- It's important for parents to store their baby's food safely to make sure they do not feed the baby spoiled food.

- Older babies will want to touch, throw, drop, and explore their food because they're very interested in learning about their environment. They will have a harder time sitting still to eat than younger babies.

- Between nine and 12 months old, a baby will be able to use a cup and will want to feed herself without help.

- A toddler's eating habits are very different than an infant's. They will probably eat fewer meals each day than they did as babies, but may like to add two or three snacks each day.

- Each day parents need to offer their toddler milk or other foods with calcium, fruits, vegetables, breads, or cereals, and meat or other protein foods. At this age, a child can eat almost all the foods that adults can eat. Their stomachs can digest food better and they have more teeth than they did as infants.

- A toddler can use a spoon, but may be very messy when eating. Babies at this age still likes to touch and play with their food. Many toddlers are less interested in their food than they were as infants. They will only want to sit at the table or in a highchair just long enough to eat the food they're interested in.

- Finger foods are small pieces of food a child can eat safely by himself. Some finger foods need special preparation by peeling, cooking, and/or cutting into small pieces.

- A baby can choke on some foods. Other foods are hard to digest, have too much sugar, or can hurt his teeth.

- Parents stop breastfeeding for many different reasons. To begin to stop, a mother could discontinue breast feeding one meal every three days. The baby can drink from a bottle or cup for the meal when not breastfeeding.

- Some parents may feel sad when they stop breast feeding. They may need extra support from their families and friends during this time.

Additional Topic Information

Things to Know First

The purpose of "Things to Know First" is to help parents recognize the influence that emotions and culture have on our attitudes toward eating and food and to offer parents ideas for making feeding times enjoyable for themselves and their baby. You can encourage parents to think carefully about how and what they feed their baby and make decisions that are best for themselves and their baby. Encourage parents to eat healthy, nutritious foods, too.

Parents and other family members play an important role in shaping children's attitudes toward food and eating. Parents also teach their children about good nutrition. It's from parents and other members of the family that children learn which foods are considered good to eat and which foods are not. They also learn which foods are associated with important family occasions and which foods have special qualities beyond satisfying hunger. For example, a particular food is good to eat when you're sick because it will help you get better.

Food not only meets the physical needs of the body, but can meet emotional needs as well. It's important to realize the connection between eating and emotions. For example, because our parents prepared food for us when we were young, we may associate eating food with love and emotional security. As children, we may have been given food to comfort us when we were upset, so now as adults we may turn to food when life is stressful. Maybe as children we were expected to eat a lot in order to show our love to the person who prepared the food. Our parents may have considered it a sign of disobedience if we did not eat, even if we were not hungry.

If parents can see the connections that have been formed between food and their emotions, they can remember that these same kinds of connections will be formed in their child, too. There may be some connections that parents do not want to be formed. For example, parents may not want their children to associate how much food they eat with how much they are loved by their parents. Or, they may not want their children to feel that in order to make their parents happy they must eat a lot of food.

Ideas about food and eating are closely tied to a person's cultural background, too. Eating is one way we celebrate life and our cultural heritage. Food takes on special meaning when it's an integral part of holidays, festivals, or other celebrations. For example, if your family served turkey and dressing at family celebrations, you may still associate turkey and dressing with family togetherness, fun, and happy feelings.

Because food and culture are closely tied, parents may experience some conflicts. Each day the parents you visit are exposed to the ideas about food through advertising. These ideas may conflict with their experience, culture, or values. Some parents may be confused because they may not be sure about the best way to feed their babies. How parents feel about these conflicts and how they deal with them will be important topics to discuss during your visits.

Two things are true about food for adults as well as children:

- Our bodies need certain types of food to stay healthy.
- Mealtimes can be enjoyable times for families to be together.

During feeding times, parents can help their baby feel like part of the family and help him learn how to feed himself, and learn what foods are good for him. Just like a baby needs to learn to walk and talk, he needs to learn to feed himself and learn how to choose nutritious foods. Feeding times are learning times for parents and their baby.

Feeding the 6- to 9-Month-Old Baby

Ideas about feeding young babies have changed over the past 30 years. In the 1950s, it was considered the "right thing to do" to start feeding a baby solid food by two months of age. Since then, research has given us better understanding of how a baby's digestive system works. Now doctors believe that a baby only needs breast milk or formula until she is six months old. Doctors have found that before six months of age a baby's system has not developed enough to properly digest the nutrients in solid food. In fact, solid food can hurt a baby's stomach. A baby may not get the nutrients he needs because he is so full from eating solid food that he doesn't eat enough breast milk or formula. He then may be at-risk for nutritional deficiencies because he is not getting what he needs.

While parents may have already begun to feed their baby solid food before six months of age, it is important that they don't feel that they have done something wrong. We just want to make sure that those parents who haven't yet begun feeding their babies solid food have this information so they can think about what they want to do for their babies.

New parents may face many different opinions about when to start feeding their baby solid foods and what foods their baby should eat first. Beginning to eat solid food is a big step for a baby as well as for her parents. A baby must learn new ways to use her mouth and tongue in order to properly chew and swallow solid food. Eating solid food is another step in the continuous process of learning how to function as a separate person. Not long after a baby begins eating solid food, she will begin to feed herself.

Parents can also learn from your visit to give their baby only one new food at a time and for three days in a row. By doing this, parents will be able to tell if their baby has any food sensitivities by watching how their baby reacts to the new food.

What should parents do if their baby does not like a particular food? If the parent is sure that the baby doesn't have a food sensitivity, they can wait a few months and try that food again. If the parent really wants the baby to learn to like the food, they can mix that food with some other food the baby does like, and each time mix in a little less of the food the baby likes. If these ideas don't work, the parent may just need to accept the fact that babies, just like adults, have different tastes and that there will be some foods that their baby just will not like to eat.

Parents may have many questions or concerns about feeding their baby the right food and making sure their baby is getting enough to eat. When a child begins to feed himself, parents may face the challenges of his growing independence. Parents may feel a little sad that they no longer will have the same closeness that they had when they were only breast or bottle-feeding. Parents may experience frustration as their child uses food to learn about their world (for example, by dropping food on the floor), or as the child begins to exercise her sense of self by refusing to eat.

Some parents may have lives that are quite stressed, emotionally, financially, or otherwise. These stresses may prevent parents from making sure their baby is getting the right kinds of foods to eat. You can discuss the difficulties they have feeding their baby and help them learn ideas for dealing with their difficulties. Good nutrition helps children get off to a good start in the world, by helping them grow strong and healthy.

As a home visitor, you can give the parents important information about what kinds of food to feed their baby and when. You also can help the parents support and encourage each other as they make and carry out decisions about feeding their child.

Feeding the 9- to 12-Month-Old Baby

When babies are 9 to 12 months old, they know what feeding time is all about. They know how to show their parents that they are hungry and ready to eat. They know that when they are put in the highchair or when they hear certain noises in the kitchen that they are going to eat soon. They know how to open their mouths and learn to get the food from a spoon.

Even though babies are better at eating and are even starting to feed themselves, their stomachs still need to have only certain kinds of food, like only breast milk or formula and not cow's milk. Babies still need to start new foods slowly, trying only one new food at a time for three days to see if they have any food sensitivities and to give them time to get used to new tastes, flavors, and textures.

Parents need to watch their baby during feeding times. By watching their baby, parents can learn a lot of things about their baby: what kind of foods they like or do not like, how long it takes them to chew and swallow food, how much food it takes to make their baby feel full, and what kinds of things distract their baby from paying attention to eating.

Some characteristics of the 9- to 12-month-old baby may make feeding time more difficult than it is with a younger baby. The 9- to 12-month-old baby is becoming more active and more interested in exploring things in the world, including food. If he hasn't already done so, he will start dropping food on the floor to see what happens, put his hands in his food to see what it feels like, and have a harder time sitting still to eat. He may want to get down right away when he is done eating.

Parents need to decide how to handle these situations. It may help if they keep in mind that babies at this age just love to explore everything in their world. They are like scientists—testing things to see how they work. Babies want to start being more involved in their own care, too, including feeding themselves. Some babies may want to feed themselves without any help from anyone. They may be very interested in what everyone else at the table is eating and want that same food.

Some parents will choose to let their baby play with their food or feed herself as much as she wants, no matter how messy she or the house gets. Other parents may choose to teach their child that food isn't something to be played with. No matter what decisions parents make, there probably will be someone who disagrees with those decisions. You can help parents sort out their thoughts and feelings about feeding their baby and offer support for those decisions, even if parents face opposition. When parents give their baby nutritious and safe foods, they are helping their baby grow and develop the best they can. How they do this is up to them.

Children of this age will have very definite likes and dislikes when it comes to food. They may refuse to try new foods, sticking to only three or four favorites. If parents are concerned that their baby may not be getting enough food, they can continue to breastfeed or bottle-feed. This is one way to make sure baby is getting enough nutrients to grow and stay healthy. Parents need to remember that because of a child's increased activity, his weight gain will slow down quite a bit. As long as a child is getting at least one "good" meal a day and several other good foods, he will develop normally and stay healthy. Of course, parents should always consult their health care provider if they're very concerned.

Feeding the Toddler

Toddlers have an increasing desire to control what happens to them, including what they eat, how much, when, and how they will eat it. This can cause difficulties for parents trying to feed a toddler. Parents may feel that their child's refusal of food is a direct challenge to the parents' authority, even though it is usually not; it's a developmental step all children make on their way to independence.

Meld's bias is that the most important thing that the parents can learn from this section is that many of the things they will see their child do are part of the normal process of development and not because the child is "bad." We do not want to discount any of the values or beliefs that parents have. However, we would like them to see how they can maintain their beliefs and still understand what is a normal and expected part of a child's development.

When a child moves from the infant stage to the toddler stage, parents may notice some changes in his eating habits. No longer does eating only meet the physical needs of the body, but it's closely tied to other aspects of the child's development. The changing needs of a toddler's body and the developing sense of autonomy, or separateness, from mother and father can affect eating habits. Understanding the reasons for changes in eating habits may help parents deal with the challenges of feeding toddlers.

Here are some things parents might notice about how their toddlers eat.

- **What parents might see**

  A toddler may eat less than when she was a baby or she may not like some of the same foods that she did before. Milk may be down to one or two cups a day. She may not like to eat vegetables, but fruits still may be accepted. Generally, toddlers eat fewer meat and protein foods, but want more bread and cereal foods.

  Reasons for this

  Physical growth and activity level have everything to do with these changes. Between birth and one year of age, a baby usually triples her weight. By her second year, there is some slowing down of the growth rate. The average toddler gains only five or six pounds between one and two years of age. A toddler tends to prefer bread and cereal foods because they are easier to handle, faster to chew, and are good for quick energy, which is needed by a toddler constantly on the go.

- **What parents might see**

  Sitting in the highchair or booster chair during an entire adult meal is practically impossible. Once the toddler is done eating, he will want to get down and get going again.

  Reasons for this

  The drive and curiosity of a toddler almost propels him to keep moving. So many things are interesting now. Food is much less interesting than it used to be. Keeping a toddler in a highchair or booster chair for more than ten minutes can be very difficult. Usually a toddler can get all the food he needs in that amount of time.

- **What parents might see**

  Toddlers do not want parents to decide what they will eat and how they will eat it. Toddlers want to make their own choices when it comes to food and eating.

Reasons for this

Becoming one's own person, that is, beginning to become separate from her mother and father, means the toddler wants to decide more and more for herself. As toddlers, children begin to make up their own minds about what they like to eat and do not like to eat, just like adults. Sometimes a toddler can be very stubborn about what she does not want to eat. If she is offered a food she doesn't like, she can push away her parent's hand with the spoon, close her mouth, or turn her head the other way. Toddlers will do all kinds of things to avoid foods they don't like.

• **What parents might see**

A child may insist on eating only one particular kind of food, like only eating bananas and no other kind of fruit or only eating chicken and no other kind of meat.

Reasons for this

Some experts suggest that often when a child makes great progress in one area, she may fall behind in another area.

If giving up the bottle or breast was easy, a child may exhibit other difficulties in eating, like only eating a particular kind of food. However, with time, these "food fads" will end.

• **What parents might see**

A toddler may make a mess at mealtimes, getting food all over himself, his chair, the floor, and everything he touches.

Reasons for this

Food is as interesting to the toddler as are other objects with which he experiments. Food can be squashed, manipulated, stacked, and dropped. The toddler doesn't see any difference between playing with his food and playing with other toys. In most cases, he isn't doing this to upset his parents or to misbehave. He is doing it because it's fun and interesting. His parents' reactions may be interesting, too.

- **What parents might see**

  "No" is the toddler's frequent response to one last spoonful or one last piece.

  Reasons for this

  The way the child learns to use words allows her to become a separate person. "No" is another dimension of deciding for herself.

- **What parents might see**

  Evening meals can be a disaster.

  Reasons for this

  Fatigue, physical growth, and changing sleep patterns may make the end of the day especially difficult for a toddler. Parents can deal with this situation in several ways. If a parent wants their toddler to eat the evening meal with the family, the toddler may need a late afternoon snack to help him wait. The toddler might eat his dinner early and then have dessert or a snack later when the rest of the family eats their meal. If the toddler has a difficult time settling down and eating a good evening meal, it may be helpful to feed him his main meal at breakfast or lunch and have a smaller meal at dinner. Serving his favorite foods at the evening meal may help, too.

The issue of power and control will probably come up over and over when you talk about feeding a toddler. If parents are feeling threatened by their child's increasing desire for independence, control, and autonomy, they can do several things to make sure that every meal doesn't become a battle of wills:

- Parents can stay in control of the situation by remembering that they make the choices when it comes to buying the foods. They can buy many different kinds of nutritious food and let their child make limited choices from among those foods. As long as parents offer their child healthy food choices, it really doesn't matter so much exactly which food a child eats or when it's eaten.

- Parents can remind themselves that their child will never starve if they're offered adequate food.

- Parents need to keep in mind that no single food is absolutely necessary. If a child doesn't like broccoli, she can eat many other kinds of vegetables.

- Parents can provide food their child can eat by himself. By doing this, the child will feel some sense of control over his eating.

- Parents can let their child eat by any method—spoon or fingers or being fed by others.

- Parents should try not to have strong rules about which foods need to be eaten first. While parents may plan what will be eaten at a meal, letting a child choose which food to eat first will give him the opportunity to exercise some control over the situation.

- Parents can let the meal end when the child has had enough to eat. Toddlers may not eat a lot at one time. They may need to eat five or six times each day. Forcing a toddler to sit in a chair and eat more food probably will lead to frustration and anger for both parent and child.

- For the most part, parents don't need to invest a lot of special time and effort in the child's meal. Because children's eating habits may be unpredictable and very changeable, putting a lot of time into preparing a meal may be frustrating for parents if the child doesn't eat much.

- Parents shouldn't use food as a reward or bribe. Children can develop bad eating habits if this is done frequently.

Here are some questions you may want to think about as you prepare to discuss the topic of feeding a toddler:

- What if parents are on a very limited budget and can only afford to buy a limited amount of food? How can parents be encouraged to choose a variety of nutritious foods for their families?

- What if parents want to teach their child that they must obey everything the parents tell them to do? How will this attitude affect power struggles over food?

- What if parents feel that a child's refusal of food is a direct challenge to their authority? How can you help parents deal with the child's normal developmental process of separating from mother and father?

- If a toddler will not eat at mealtime, should she be "punished" by not getting something to eat a little later when she is hungry?

These questions are for you to think about in terms of how you personally may have handled similar situations and how you might respond when they arise in a visit. These questions relate to both economic and cultural issues. Your discussions can be a wonderful place for the parents to think about and make decisions regarding their child's eating.

Food Ideas

Finger foods are usually bite-size and don't need to be eaten with a spoon or fork. Finger foods are fun for children to eat and often are fun for adults, too. Often we think of them as "snack" foods, but a young child can eat an entire meal of finger foods.

Finger foods are good because they allow a child the opportunity to feed herself. This helps develop her sense of personal competence because she has learned a new skill and she doesn't need parents or others to help her eat. Finger foods allow her to use her fingers in a way that develops the small muscles in her hands. The development of these small muscles is important because they are the same muscles she will use later to hold a spoon or fork or write with a pencil.

When parents give their child finger foods, they need to make sure the foods are safe. As with all foods, a child should try only one new finger food at a time so parents can check for food sensitivities. Parents need to make sure that their child can chew and swallow the food safely. Parents will need to do special preparation (such as cutting, peeling, or cooking) with some foods before a young child can eat them as finger foods. Some foods are particularly dangerous because a young child can choke on them very easily. These foods need to be avoided altogether until the child is three years old. Examples of these foods are popcorn, nuts, seeds, and raw carrots.

Parents can take an active role in their child's health and nutrition by making baby food. Parents can control how fresh the food is, how it's cooked, and what goes into it. This can be a good way for parents to feel proud of what they do for their child. However, we don't want parents to feel guilty if they don't have the time or desire to make their own baby food. It can be easy for parents to feel like they're not doing all they can for their child and we certainly don't want to contribute to those feelings. The reality of some parents' lives may be that this kind of activity is just not possible. And that is okay! We just want to offer some different ways parents can be active participants in their child's nutrition.

At your visit you can have fun with the topics of "Finger Foods" and "Making Baby Food." Get everyone involved in a lot of hands-on experiences!

How to Stop Breastfeeding

Making the decision to stop breastfeeding can be easy for some parents, hard for others. The reasons for stopping are many. Some mothers stop breastfeeding because they want to stop. They may feel that they've gotten their baby off to a good nutritional start and now want the freedom that comes when others in the family can share the responsibility of feeding their baby.

Some mothers stop breastfeeding because of other things going on in their lives—like the need to go to work or school. Some stop because their baby is having a hard time getting the amount of food he needs from the breast. These parents choose to stop breastfeeding and put their baby on infant formula to make sure their baby grows well and stays healthy. No matter what the reason for stopping, many mothers miss the special closeness they felt with their baby during breastfeeding.

For some parents, the decision to stop may not be as hard to make as the decision **when** to stop. They may have mixed feelings about stopping. They may desire the freedom that weaning will bring, but they may be afraid to give up that special closeness they feel when they're breastfeeding or they may have a problem paying the additional money that will be needed to buy infant formula.

Some parents may feel guilty if they think they are stopping too soon or too late. They may feel pressure from others to do it a different way instead of the way that they themselves want to do it. Your visit can be an excellent time to talk about these feelings and to share ideas about dealing with the difficulties that may arise.

When the weaning process begins, parents need to do it slowly, both for the sake of the mother's body and to help their child adjust to the change. A mother's breasts need time to get used to the smaller and smaller amounts of milk that are taken by her child. By weaning gradually, mothers will not experience as much breast pain as they would if they just stopped completely in one day. If a baby hasn't been fed from a bottle or cup before, it might take him a little while to be willing to give up the breast and to learn new ways to drink.

When changing from breastfeeding to bottle-feeding, parents should try to keep the routine the same as much as possible. Hold the baby when giving her a bottle. Mothers might try expressing a little breast milk and feeding it to the baby from a bottle or cup to help their baby get used to drinking from the bottle or cup. Parents need to make sure that their child is still getting enough milk so that they continue to stay healthy and grow strong.

Learning to drink from a bottle or cup is another step in the process of the baby's learning to become a separate person from their mother. Parents can be proud of their child making the transition from breast to bottle or cup.

As you prepare for your visit, you can find the additional information about breastfeeding and bottle-feeding in parenting information book *Baby Is Here!* If the parents have not been bottle-feeding along with breastfeeding, it may be a good idea to cover the topic of bottle-feeding either after or along with the topic of stopping breastfeeding.

Concerns to Be Aware of During Home Visits

If you notice any of these things, discuss them with the parents and/or your supervisor. Your supervisor will help you decide what needs to be done.

- Parents having a lot of trouble dealing with cultural or family conflicts about feeding their baby.
- Parents thinking that feeding time is not very important to their baby.
- Parents having a lot of trouble feeding their baby.
- Parents seeming to have trouble feeding their baby solid food.
- Parents having a lot of trouble making sure their baby gets nutritious food.

- A baby that seems to be hungry all the time.

- A baby that doesn't look healthy.

- Parents not seeming to care what kind of food they feed their baby.

- Parents feeling their baby is "bad" because he makes a mess with his food or because he wants to start feeding himself.

- Parents having trouble feeding their toddlers.

- Parents giving their child finger foods that aren't safe or aren't good for her.

- Parents giving their child nuts, popcorn, seeds, or raw carrots before they're old enough to chew them well.

- Parents not thinking it's important to know how to properly store baby food.

- Parents thinking it's not important to know how to stop breastfeeding so that it's easiest for mother and baby.

- Parents having a very difficult time stopping breastfeeding.

- A baby that is not getting enough to eat after stopping breastfeeding.

Things to Know First

Things to Know First

Getting Ready

Agenda

- **Opening:** families and food
- **Keeping It Going:** mealtime traditions
- **Closing:** using what we've learned

Objectives

Parents will

- discuss the importance of food and eating to families and children
- learn their baby's eating habits and the signals that show he is hungry or full
- understand that a healthy diet is important for their baby's growth and development

In Advance

- Review the information in the parenting information book *Feeding Your Child.*

Materials

Activity 1: Food and Culture

- *Young Family Parenting Information* book *Feeding Your Child* for parents
- information about WIC or other nutrition programs

Activity 2: Feeding Time

- Polaroid or other camera with instant developing or another camera and film

Things to Know First

Opening

"Are there special foods that your family eats at certain times—birthdays, holidays, Sundays, or other times? How do the parents think these special foods came about in the family? Were they passed down from grandparents or others? Are they a part of their religious tradition?"

Keeping It Going

Activity 1: Food and Culture

Involve parents in a discussion of how food is part of their families' lives and traditions. Prompt the discussion about the role food plays in families with questions like these:

- How do the parents feel about these traditions surrounding food?
- Do they think such traditions are important? Why or why not?

Families and friends are often full of advice about how to feed babies. Ask the parents what their parents or others have told them about when to feed their baby, what to feed her, how much, and any other feeding advice they have gotten. Do they need or want this advice? How do parents respond to all this input?

Discuss how this advice might be full of contradictions or may even be wrong, based on what we know now from nutritionists and their research. How can parents figure out what to do?

Brainstorm some ideas on where to get accurate information. Here are some ideas:

- from their health care professional
- from up-to-date books, web sites, or magazines at the library

what are some of your food traditions?

MINE:
1. MAKE SOMETHING EVERYONE LIKES TO THEIR LIKING.
2. ALWAYS HAVE VEGGIES.
3. ALWAYS TRY SOMETHING DIFFERENT.
4. NEVER EAT ALONE.

- from nutritionists at their clinic
- from government agencies and programs such as WIC (Women, Infants, and Children nutrition program)

Ask parents how they handle it when others give them advice about feeding their baby that they don't want to follow. You and the parents can role play ways to respond to advice in a firm, assertive way without being defensive or argumentative.

What are some things parents can say when someone says, for example, "Why does that baby still have a bottle?" or other comments? Here are some things they could say:

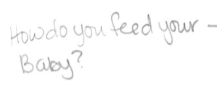

Check w/ Doctor

- My doctor says it's okay for her to have one bottle day. (Or whatever their health care professional did say.)
- Thanks for your concern and advice.

Activity 2: Feeding Time

Ask the parents where they usually feed their baby.
Have the baby join you and the parents. If your visit is at the time they usually feed their baby, ask if it is okay to observe feeding time.

How do you feed your Baby?

Go over the parenting information on what makes a comfortable feeding time for baby.
Ask the parents to begin feeding their baby. While they are feeding, ask them to try ideas like these:

- Have the parents give their baby their full attention while feeding him. After a bit, ask them to keep feeding their baby but to pay attention to something else, such as a TV show or a conversation with you.

- You talk to the baby while he is eating. Keep talking while the parents try to feed him.

- Show the baby a toy while she is eating.

- Ask the parents to try to keep feeding the baby after he is full.

Having the baby sit while eating is an important safety measure. Many children choke as a result of eating while walking around.

Discuss how the baby reacted to each of these different things.
When did the baby eat the best? How did he act when they showed him the toy? What about the talking? Did that distract him?

Ask parents to think about what conditions make the baby most comfortable while he is eating.
How do the parents think they are doing in making feeding time special for them and their baby? Are there things they can improve that would make the time more fun and/or relaxing for them and the baby? Help the parents brainstorm some ideas and practice these ideas during this feeding.

Here are some ideas for parents to try with their baby:

- Turn off the TV.
- Be sure the baby has a comfortable spot to sit (if appropriate) and eat.
- Focus on feeding, not playing.
- Don't rush.

Ask parents what their favorite foods and beverages are, especially for snacks.

Baby & Their's

You can share your favorites, too. Many adults choose sweets, salty snacks, pop, and other "junk" foods. Few choose carrots and water as their first choices. Remind parents that it is okay for adults who eat a healthy diet to indulge in these treats every so often, but that babies need healthy food because they are growing and changing so fast.

Ask if you can take their baby's picture while she is eating.
Often parents think a picture of a messy baby is cute. Others may want to clean their baby up or pose with him. Give the family the pictures or, at your next visit, bring the pictures of the baby for the family to keep.

Talk to the parents about different foods that are appropriate for babies and toddlers to eat.
Some foods are dangerous for young babies and toddlers. Others aren't good for babies to eat because they don't help baby grow.

Take a tour of the refrigerator and cupboards with the parents.
Look for foods that could cause choking such as candy, hot dogs, grapes, popcorn, and tortilla chips. Encourage the parents to be careful around babies and toddlers whenever foods like these are served to older kids or adults.

Take a "sweets" inventory, too.
Babies can only eat so much a day, and every bite needs to count. Babies should not eat foods like candy, cookies, pop, or other "junk" foods. These foods can fill baby up and she won't eat the good food she needs.

Be sure it is okay with the parents to do the cupboard and refrigerator tour. This isn't an "inspection" to find out what they eat or feed their baby, but a means to talk about what makes a safe and healthy food for their baby.

During the tour, make positive comments about the healthy snacks and foods (for parents and children) you find.

Encourage the parents to feed their child healthy foods and to consider their own diets, too, since as the baby grows, he will want to eat what his parents eat.

Activity 3: Learning about Your Child

Babies and young children know when they are hungry and when they are full, but they can't say this in words. Even when they can talk, they may not always know what they are feeling is hunger. Ask the parents to describe a hungry baby—any hungry baby.

Then ask the parents to describe how their baby acts when she is hungry. How do they know their baby is finished eating? There are some clues in the parenting information book.

Ask the parents what they have observed about their child's eating habits.
Does he like to try new foods? What are her favorite foods? What time of day is he most likely to be hungry? Are the baby's eating habits similar to mom's or dad's? In what ways?

Go over the questions in the parenting information book in the "Learning about Your Child" section.
Ask the parents how this information can help them during mealtimes or other times.

Parents with children of different ages may feel they're running a restaurant as they prepare different foods for different children. You can help parents work out menus and find foods that work for the whole family. Affirm parents for all they do for all their children to keep them fed and happy.

Closing

Help parents summarize what they learned by going over these points. You may want to add others if you notice parents need more information.

- ✓ All adults and children need certain types of food to be healthy.

- ✓ Families can be full of information and advice about feeding children. Not all of their information and advice is accurate or helpful. Parents can decide what to feed and how to feed their own children.

- ✓ Parents can learn to recognize when baby is hungry or full and her likes and dislikes about food by watching her eat.

Feeding Your
6- to 9-Month-Old Baby

Feeding Your
6- to 9-Month-Old Baby

Getting Ready

Agenda

- **Opening:** what young babies eat
- **Keeping It Going:** introducing solid foods
- **Closing:** using what we've learned

Objectives

Parents will

- learn what babies eat at this age
- learn how to introduce new foods to their baby
- know what foods to avoid for babies under one year

In Advance

- Review the information in Chapter 2 of the parenting information book *Feeding Your Child.*

Materials

Activity 1: Milk and Other Foods

- Young Family Parenting Information book *Feeding Your Child* for parents
- infant "sippy" cup, infant spoon, bowls, measuring spoons, ready-made formula
- several varieties of infant cereal
- Jars of baby foods for young babies that contain one kind of food. Bring different brands of the same variety, like peas or pears.
- Jars of baby foods for older babies, sometimes called toddler foods. These have more than one type of food in them, like chicken and noodles.
- pages from the parenting information book on what to feed a 6- to 9-month-old baby

Getting Ready (continued)

Activity 2: Calendars and Menus
- copy of the "Calendars and Menus for Introducing New Foods" handout in the parenting information book
- pen or pencil

Feeding Your 6- to 9-Month-Old Baby

Opening

"Until a baby is six months old, she only needs breast milk or formula to eat. This gives her all the nutrition she needs. At six months old, parents can start feeding their baby solid foods. The first solid food a baby will try is baby rice cereal mixed with breast milk or formula."

Keeping It Going

Activity 1: Milk and Other Foods

Quickly review the information in parent book *Feeding Your Child* about feeding 6- to-9-month-old babies.
Remind the parents that babies only need breast milk or formula until they are six months old. Depending on the age of the baby, work with the parents using the menu chart in *Feeding Your Child*.

Go over the pages that show different kinds of foods that a young baby can eat.
Discuss which of these foods, if any, their baby has tried. Has their baby had any reactions to the foods? If so, what kind of reaction? What did the parents do? Remind the parents to discuss any reaction to foods with their health care provider.

Remind the parents that it is important for them to know what is in all food their baby eats.
Show the parents how to read the labels on the baby food jars.

Point out the jars that contain only one kind of meat, vegetable, or fruit.
These jars containing only one food are the ones to serve a baby 6 to 9 months old.

The mixed foods aren't good until a baby is older. Parents can't know how much of each type of food is in the jar. If their baby does have an allergic reaction, they wouldn't know which of the foods in the jar caused it.

What you do in a visit about feeding a baby will obviously depend on the age of the child. Talk to the parents to see what questions they have about feeding.

Look at the labels again.
Does the food contain anything else, like salt? Remind the parents not to feed their baby foods containing salt or other additives or preservatives. Babies don't need salt or spices and some additives can cause reactions. Pure foods are best.

Activity 2: Calendars and Menus

Help the parents plan what their baby will eat.
Go over the calendars for introducing new foods in the parent book. The calendars will help the parents slowly introduce new foods to their babies.

Point out that a baby just beginning to eat solid foods begins with rice cereal mixed with breast milk or formula.
Rice cereal is the mildest; few babies have a *food sensitivity* (bad reaction to the food) to rice cereal.

Show parents how to mix the cereal.
Breast milk or formula may be warm or cold, depending on what the baby likes. If the parents have a microwave, warn them about using it to heat their baby's food or formula. Microwaves do not heat foods evenly; the foods could have hot spots that could burn their baby's mouth.

Point out the progress their baby will make in eating solid food by using the menu chart.
Parents should feed cereal only for the first two to three weeks. Then they can add one-half jar of any single fruit at the midday meal. Remind the parents to feed their baby only one new food at a time to see if he has a sensitivity to it.

If the baby is already eating solid food, ask the parents to write down as much as they can remember of their baby's menu for the last few days.
Compare the baby's diet with what is recommended in the parenting information book. Do the parents need to add or take away anything from their baby's menu? Remind the parents that they haven't hurt their baby by feeding things not on the menu, but suggest they substitute the recommended items in their baby's diet.

Siblings will want to try to feed the baby, too. Encourage the parents to let them participate after the parents have taught them how to gently and carefully feed the baby only the foods the baby can eat. Remind the parents to supervise at all times.

Be sure to praise the parents for doing their best in feeding their baby a healthy diet.

Closing

Help parents summarize what they learned by going over these points. You may want to add others if you notice parents need more information.

- ✓ Infants under six months old need to eat only breast milk or formula.
- ✓ Parents can introduce rice cereal at around six months and gradually add other solid foods like other kinds of cereal, fruit, and vegetables.
- ✓ 6- to 9-month-old babies should eat baby food that contains only one kind of food at a time.

Feeding Your
9- to 12-Month-Old Baby

Feeding Your
9- to 12-Month-Old Baby

Agenda

- **Opening:** baby's favorite foods
- **Keeping It Going:** food for your growing baby
- **Closing:** using what we've learned

Objectives

Parents will

- learn what babies eat at this age
- learn how to introduce new foods to their baby

In Advance

- Review the information in Chapter 3 of the parenting information book *Feeding Your Child.*

Materials

Activity 1: Milk and Other Foods

- Young Family Parenting Information book *Feeding Your Child* for parents
- infant "sippy" cup, infant spoon, bowls, measuring spoons, ready-made formula
- several varieties of infant cereal
- Jars of baby foods for young babies that contain one kind of food. Bring different brands of the same variety, like peas or pears.
- Jars of baby foods for older babies, sometimes called toddler foods. These have more than one type of food in them, like chicken and noodles.
- pages from the parenting information book on what to feed a 9- to 12-month-old baby
- Polaroid or other camera with instant developing or another camera and film

Getting Ready (continued)

Activity 2: Sample Feeding Schedule

- Young Family Parenting Information book *Feeding Your Child* for parents
- copy of My Baby's Eating Schedule handout at the end of this section
- pen or pencil

Feeding Your
9- to 12-Month-Old Baby

Opening

"Babies this age are beginning to eat more and varied foods. It is still important to introduce only one new food at a time, in case your baby has a reaction to the food. Babies are interested in using their hands, too, so introducing finger foods is a good idea now."

Keeping It Going

Activity 1: Milk and Other Foods

Review the information in the parent book on feeding 9- to-12-month-old babies.

Now that the baby is older, she can start to eat different foods. Junior foods are for older babies because they aren't as smooth as baby foods. Babies can use their muscles and tongues with junior foods. This helps develop those muscles for talking.

Most babies are interested in feeding themselves by this age. It can be quite entertaining to watch a baby eat by himself. If the parents have not started to let their baby feed himself, encourage them to do so.

With the parents okay, set their baby up in the high chair or wherever the baby usually eats.

Give the baby the sippy cup (cup with two handles and a lid) and show him how to use it. Then stand back and watch. What does the baby do? Can he figure it out? Ask the parents how they would teach their baby to use the cup.

Offer the baby a spoon and a bowl of soft food like cottage cheese.

Can the baby handle the spoon? Probably not yet, but he will figure out how to pick up the food with his fingers or hands. Encourage the parents to let their baby feed himself during part of each meal.

Ask the parents if you can take the baby's picture while the baby is eating or when he is finished.

Often parents think a picture of a messy baby is cute. They may want to clean the baby up or pose with him. That's okay, too. Leave the pictures with the parents or bring them at your next visit.

You can use the activity on making baby food at home if that is appropriate for these parents and the child's age.

Consider doing the finger food activity in the "Ideas to Help" topic as part of this one. This age is a good time to introduce finger foods.

Activity 2: Sample Feeding Schedule

Ask the parents to fill in My Baby's Eating Schedule.

Ask parents to write down as much as they can remember of their baby's menu for the last day or two.
Compare the baby's diet with what is recommended in the parent book. Do the parents need to add or take away anything from their baby's menu? Remind the parents that they haven't hurt their baby by feeding things not on the menu, but suggest they substitute the recommended items in their baby's diet.

Suggest that the parents continue to introduce only one food at a time in case their baby has a reaction to a food.
Keeping notes about what their baby has eaten can help parents narrow it down to one food if the baby does have a reaction. Encourage the parents to discuss with their health care provider any bad reaction their baby has to a food.

Closing

Help parents summarize what they learned by going over these points. You may want to add others if you notice that parents need more information.

- ✓ Around nine months, babies are interested in and able to handle finger foods like Cheerios or Kix. Babies like to pick up these foods and feed themselves.
- ✓ Not all finger foods are appropriate for babies. They can choke on some foods that are small, brittle, or have sharp edges, like tortilla chips.
- ✓ Parents should continue to introduce new foods one at a time in case their baby has a sensitivity or reaction to a new food.

Feeding Your Toddler
(1 to 3 Years Old)

Feeding Your Toddler (1 to 3 Years Old)

Agenda

- **Opening:** changing tastes for food
- **Keeping It Going:** toddlers' nutrition needs
- **Closing:** using what we've learned

Objectives

Parents will

- understand that toddlers have different nutrition needs as they grow
- learn tips to help their toddler eat what he needs

In Advance

- Review the information in Chapter 4 of the parenting information book *Feeding Your Child.*

Materials

Activity 1: Feeding Your Toddler

- Young Family Parenting Information book *Feeding Your Child* for parents
- copy of the How Much to Feed Your Toddler handout at the end of this section
- Pictures of foods or the actual foods in the five food groups—dairy foods, meat and protein, fruits and vegetables, breads and cereals, and fats. You may also want to use a food pyramid, which shows how a diet should be built on quantities of different foods.
- Polaroid or other camera with instant developing or another camera and film

Activity 2: Tips for Toddlers

- drawing paper
- markers or crayons

Feeding Your Toddler
(1 to 3 Years Old)

Opening

"Toddlers start to show their increasing independence and desire to control themselves and their surroundings at mealtimes. They may develop ideas about food, such as only eating certain things or not wanting food to touch other food. This is normal. Parents just need to be sure their child is eating enough and eating nutritious food."

Keeping It Going

Activity 1: Feeding Your Toddler

Quickly review the feeding toddlers information in the parenting information book.
Toddlers eat differently than babies. They can eat more and varied foods because they have more teeth and can chew different foods. Toddlers' stomachs are able to deal with different foods, too.

Use the parent book's sample menus for younger babies to compare how babies and toddlers eat. If the parents have a younger or older child than the child that is the focus of this visit, ask the parents how that child's eating habits and needs are different than this child's. Or, you can talk about how this baby's eating habits have changed as he has grown. How do these differences affect what the parents prepare for family meals?

You can do the activity on finger foods in the "Ideas to Help" topic with parents of toddlers, too.

Ask the parents how much their toddler seems to be eating.
Using the How Much to Feed Your Toddler handout, ask the parents to record what their toddler has been eating. Ask them to include the amounts, as close as they can remember. Review the Sample Eating Schedule for Your Toddler in the parenting information book. How does the menu compare to the one the parents wrote down?

Ask the parents if you can take their baby's picture while their baby is eating or when he is finished.
Often parents think a picture of a messy baby is cute. The parents may want to clean their baby up or pose with him. That's okay, too. Leave the pictures with the parents or bring them on your next visit.

If the parents are worried, suggest they keep a list of everything their child eats for a week. If they look at the big picture—not just one or two meals—they may feel better about their child's eating habits.

Ask the parents what they have done to be sure their child is eating right.
Getting the right amounts and the right kinds of food into toddlers can be a struggle. Toddlers want to be in charge of themselves, including what they eat. Is the toddler that lives here like that?

Use the pictures of the food and the suggested serving sizes to plan some toddler meals. Do several days' worth of meals this way and write the menus down.

Activity 2: Tips for Toddlers

Give the parents the paper and crayons or markers.
Ask the parents to draw a picture or write down two things their toddler is doing when eating. One could be something their child is learning, like how to use a spoon. The other could be being humorous or frustrating, like dropping food on the floor or "painting" with food on the high chair tray. Talk about how different mealtime with a toddler is now than it was with a breast or bottle-feeding infant or a younger baby.

Remind the parents that food fights—where a child doesn't want to eat, only wants to eat one food, won't eat when food is served, or disagree over food in any number of other ways—are common between parents and toddlers.
These things can be tough to handle. Talk about why toddlers act this way.

- Toddlers want to feed themselves. It shows they are becoming independent.

- Toddlers like the security of sameness and may choose to eat only foods they have had before.

- A toddlers' eating schedule might be different from other family members'.

- Toddlers find it fun to make messes.

Brainstorm ways to handle some of these issues.
Here are some ideas:

- Don't fight it—let your child eat only one food for awhile, as long as she seems healthy.

- Use a big plastic tablecloth under your toddler's chair to make cleanup easier.

- Encourage independence by serving foods your toddler can feed himself.

- If your toddler doesn't like milk, serve foods that contain milk like pudding, cheese, or frozen yogurt.

- Use the toddlers' love of snacks to serve healthy foods— small bites of meat, slices of banana, orange sections, strips of bread with peanut butter.

Review the tips for helping toddlers eat.
Remind the parents that it is not easy to avoid mealtime struggles, but it is possible to make the mealtime more pleasant for both the parents and child. Planning and preparation can help parents avoid struggles over food.

Closing

Help parents summarize what they learned by going over these points. You may want to add others if you notice parents need more information.

- ✓ Toddlers may show their growing independence by fussing about food. They may want to eat only one or two foods. Many toddlers like to make messes with food. Some toddlers even refuse to eat. All of this is normal. Parents just need to make sure that their toddler is getting enough to eat over a period of several days.

- ✓ Knowing how their toddler reacts to food and eating in different situations can make it easier to avoid "food fights" between the parents and their child.

> Reinforce to parents that as long as their child seems healthy and is developing well, they don't need to be overly concerned about their toddler's diet. Encourage them to look at what their child eats over several days, rather than only at one meal.

Ideas to Help

Ideas to Help

Agenda

- **Opening:** finger foods for toddlers
- **Keeping It Going:** preparing finger foods and baby food
- **Closing:** using what we've learned

Objectives

Parents will

- be introduced to finger foods to children old enough to eat them
- learn how to make baby food at home

In Advance

- Review the information in Chapter 5 of the parenting information book *Feeding Your Child.*

Materials

Activity 1: Finger Foods

- Young Family Parenting Information book *Feeding Your Child* for parents
- simple finger foods—Cheerios or Kix, fresh or frozen peas. (See Chapter 5 for more examples.)
- fingers foods that need preparation before being given to babies or toddlers — cheese, soft tortillas, apple, banana, pear
- finger foods that must be cooked and cut into pieces before being served — potato, egg yolks, carrots

Activity 2: Making Baby Food

- baby food grinder or blender
- simple foods that can be made into baby food like bananas, cooked vegetables, or cooked meats

Ideas to Help

Opening

"Finger foods are a big part of older babies' and toddlers' diets. Many are good for a baby and encourage small motor development, but we need to avoid certain kinds of foods that can cause choking. Parents can learn to make healthy baby food at home, using foods they eat."

Keeping It Going

Activity 1: Finger Foods

Show parents some of the finger foods you brought that are quick and simple.
Older babies (and toddlers) love finger foods because they can pick them up and eat them. Put the baby in the high chair and give her some Cheerios or Kix. Does she like them?

Watch the baby eat the finger foods.
Encourage the parents to talk about the importance of letting their baby feed himself.

Here are some reasons finger foods are important:

- feeding themselves encourages independence and learning

- babies enjoy the exploration and play of finger foods

- picking up small foods with their fingers encourages small motor development

Show the parents some of the other foods that need more preparation.
Chapter 5 of the parent book has some finger food ideas and ways to prepare them. Let the parents prepare one or two of the foods you brought, such as the cheese or tortilla.

Parents may be reluctant to serve finger foods because they can be messy. Encourage the parents to find ways to include finger foods because they are important to their baby's development.
Suggest that they serve finger foods only when their baby is in a high chair or other more controlled environment to help prevent choking.

Point out the finger foods that can be dangerous and remind the parents to beware whenever these foods are around their baby.
Nuts, popcorn, hot dogs, string cheese, grapes, peanut butter on a spoon, raisins, and other foods can cause choking. Other foods, like corn, baked beans, chocolate, onion, and potato chips, can cause stomach upsets in some babies. Avoid serving any of these foods to young children.

Activity 2: Making Baby Food

Show the parents how they can make their own baby foods from foods they eat.
Commercial or store bought baby foods are convenient and easy to get, but they can be expensive. Some parents may be interested in making their own baby food so they know what their baby is eating and/or can reduce the expense.

Demonstrate how to use the baby food grinder or blender you brought.
Remind the parents of these things:

- Wash your hands and foods before any cooking or preparation.

- Use clean plastic bags or other containers such as ice cube trays or muffin tins for storage.

- Do not add salt, spices, or sugar to food used for the baby. Babies don't need these in their diets.

- Don't feed your baby from the jar or container. Put the food into a bowl so food left in the jar doesn't become contaminated during feeding.

- Use leftover food within 24 hours, even if it is refrigerated. Storing food longer than that may cause the food to spoil.

Let parents try the baby food grinder or blender.
Take an inventory of any leftovers or fruits and vegetables the parents may have on hand. Can any of these be made into baby food? If so, use those. Otherwise, use the food you brought with you.

Review the pages on making food for a baby in the parenting information book.
The important thing to remember is to keep everything clean during preparation, including washing vegetables and fruits and using clean utensils. Baby food should be frozen or refrigerated immediately and kept that way until serving. Remind the parents to warm foods on the stove, not in a microwave. Microwaves can heat unevenly and cause hot spots in the food, which can burn their baby.

Closing

Help parents summarize what they learned by going over these points. You may want to add others if you notice parents need more information.

- ✓ Parents can make wholesome, healthy baby food at home using many of the foods they would normally eat. It is important to maintain a clean kitchen and utensils to keep food safe.

- ✓ Babies and toddlers like finger foods. These can be a big part of their diets after about nine months. Parents need to be careful to avoid giving their baby certain finger foods that could cause choking.

Handouts

My Baby's Eating Schedule

	What Time Does Your Child Usually Eat?	**What Do You Feed Your Child?**
Early Morning		
Middle Morning		
Lunch		
Middle Afternoon		
Dinner		
Before Bed or Night		

How Much to Feed Your Toddler

Milk and Milk Foods

Each day your child needs 2 1/2 cups.

Meats and Protein Foods

Each day your child needs 2 ounces of meat OR 2 ounces of protein food.

Vegetables and Fruits

Each day your child needs 1/4 cup from the Vitamin A list AND 1/2 cup from the Vitamin C list AND 1/4 cup from the Others list. (See page 61.)

Breads and Cereals

Each day your child needs 2 1/2 servings.

Chapter 3
Healthy Child/Sick Child

Keeping Well

Sick Child

Introduction

Home Visitor Information

Keeping children healthy can be a challenge. Adults and children are exposed to germs everyday, everywhere they go. You don't want to get parents so worried that they become fearful, but you can introduce ways parents can help their children stay well. These include getting regular well-child checkups, keeping immunizations up-to-date, taking some easy steps to help avoid germs, and doing regular checks for changes in baby's sight, hearing, and teeth. The *Healthy Child/Sick Child* book also includes ways to ease the discomfort of a sick child and to help parents be prepared for when their child does get sick.

There are several pieces of information and handouts in this section that are not in the Young Family Parenting Information book *Healthy Child/ Sick Child*. These are the hand-washing demonstration and handout, and the tooth-care section. You can leave the handouts with parents to supplement the information in the Young Family book.

After the activities in *Healthy Child/Sick Child*, parents will

- understand the importance of well-child checkups and immunizations

- know what happens at a well-child checkup

- know the recommended immunizations schedule

- know how to prepare for their well-child doctor's visit

- understand how children get sick

- know simple things they can do to keep their child from getting sick

- understand the importance of checking their child's sight, hearing, and teeth

- be prepared for their child's illness

- know how to take their child's axillary (underarm) temperature

- recognize symptoms of illness

- know when to call their health care provider and what to say

- know how to give their baby medicine
- know ways to help their baby and themselves feel better when baby is sick
- recognize symptoms of common childhood illnesses
- know how to care a child sick with a common illness

Important Information for Home Visitors

- Checkups are regularly scheduled visits to a health care provider that help parents to take good care of their baby. Checkups can help find problems parents can't see and show parents the new things their baby can do. At a checkup, a baby may get an immunization, which prevents some kinds of diseases.

- It helps if the parents have learned ways to communicate with their health care professional. If possible, parents should take their baby to the same health care provider each time for checkups.

- Parents can do a lot to help keep their baby healthy. Regular hand washing is one very important step and can help prevent the spread of germs that cause many illnesses.

- When parents call their health care provider, they need to clearly and carefully tell the staff the baby's symptoms (how the baby acts, his temperature, any vomiting, changes in eating, bowel movements or urinating, rashes, and more).

- It can be difficult for parents to know if their baby's hearing is okay. To check, parents must watch their baby closely. If the baby notices noises and likes toys or other objects that make sounds, then his hearing is probably okay. Parents should also watch their baby carefully to be sure that her sight is okay. Tell the baby's health professional about any concerns regarding hearing or sight.

- Parents can discuss with their dentist when their child should have her first dental checkup. Even baby teeth need to be taken care of by brushing and visits to the dentist.

- Parents can do many things to be prepared for when their baby does get sick. Parents should know how to get help and have important phone numbers for their health care provider and drugstore in a place where they can quickly find them. It is important to have basic medicines and first-aid supplies on hand and know how to take a baby's temperature. Before giving medicine to their baby, parents need to read and follow the directions on the bottle very carefully.

- Babies can't easily tell parents when they are sick. Parents must watch their baby closely to know.

- It takes a lot of time for parents to care for a sick baby. When parents have been taking care of their sick baby for a few days, they may feel tired and frustrated. Parents need to take care of themselves and consider getting help from others. It may help parents care for their sick baby if they remember that most illnesses are only temporary.

- Each physical problem has specific signs called *symptoms*. If parents know the signs, they can watch for them when they think their baby might be sick.

- For many illnesses, there are things parents can do at home to help their baby feel better and get well. Parents need to learn when they should call their health care provider or emergency room for help.

- When babies are sick, they need even more attention and love from their parents.

Additional Topic Information

During the first few years of life, parents need to take their baby to their health care provider for regular checkups and shots according to a schedule. At the checkup, a health professional can find out if the baby is growing normally and seems healthy, as well as spot any problems the baby might have. If a baby has a problem, they can try things to help correct the problem and tell the parents how to keep the problem from happening again. If a baby does get sick, parents can be prepared with some supplies and information to help their baby feel better.

Checkups and Immunizations

To grow and develop, children need to be healthy. The two most important things that parents can do to keep their child healthy are to

- take their child for regular checkups
- make sure their child receives her immunizations on schedule

Although these may seem like very simple things, they can be hard for parents who have very stressful lives, don't see the need for regular checkups or immunizations, or are afraid to go to their health care provider. There can be other barriers, too, including limited access or limited money.

A child's health is probably one of the greatest concerns of any parent. While parents need to realize that they are responsible for their child's health and health care, they must understand that there are many things that they can do to keep their child healthy, too.

Immunizations given on a preplanned schedule protect babies from diseases such as polio, mumps, measles, diphtheria, pertussis (whooping cough), and tetanus. Some of these diseases can kill babies if they're not protected against them. That is why it's so important for parents to take their baby for checkups so he can get his immunizations.

Parents need to understand how their health care provider works. Because so many people come to the office or clinic each day for regular checkups and small problems, **parents need to make an appointment.** An appointment will help make sure that each person will get to see the health care provider.

Even with an appointment, sometimes parents must wait a while to see their health care provider in a busy office. Even if parents think they will need to wait, they should still get to the office or clinic on time for their appointments. You can encourage parents to be prepared in case they will need to wait. Parents can bring food or toys to help keep their child entertained while waiting to see their health professional.

Parents can make an appointment on the phone or they can schedule their child's next appointment when they're at the office. You can help parents to see the need to get a calendar and mark down every appointment. Parents should call if they will not be able to keep the appointment and reschedule it right away. Remind the parents how busy the office can be so they should try to keep the appointment, otherwise it may be awhile before they can get in again.

It's important for parents to take their baby to the same health care provider for their checkups. When parents take their baby in for regular checkups, the doctor or nurse writes down his height, weight, and other important medical information. By going to the same health care provider, parents make sure that the health care provider has all the information about their baby. This information is used to keep track of the baby's development and to identify any health problems that he may have.

Parents should take their child to the emergency room when their baby is seriously ill or hurt. For less serious problems, such as a fever, cold or the flu, it is better to wait until the health care provider's office is open for business. In most cases, parents will need an appointment. For more information about when parents **should** take their baby to the emergency room, see parent information book *Safe Child and Emergencies*.

Health care providers can give parents much information about their baby. They can tell parents if their baby is healthy and growing and developing at a normal rate. The health professional can tell the parents how their baby will change and what the baby might do in the coming months (like crawling, walking, or talking). They can answer questions parents might have about their baby's eating, sleeping, or crying.

During the physical examination, some babies get upset because they are touched, moved, undressed, or woken up. Parents need to know that this is okay, that their baby isn't being hurt. The baby is just a little uncomfortable. However, there are things that parents can do to help their baby feel less upset. They can talk softly to their baby, rub the baby gently in a place that the health professional isn't examining, or ask if they can hold their baby while he is being examined.

Sometimes health care providers get very busy and don't take the time to ask the parents if they have any questions. Encourage the parents to ask their health care provider questions even if they are a little afraid. Help parents learn how to write down their questions before the appointment, tell the health care provider at the **beginning** of the appointment that they have some questions, and then make sure they get answers to all of their questions **after** the examination.

Health care providers know a lot of medical information that is hard for others to understand. Sometimes when medical personnel answer questions they may use medical words parents may not know. Parents need to keep asking questions until they get answers they can understand. Parents can exercise certain "rights" in the care of their child at the office or clinic. Parents need to be informed about health care so that they know their rights and can be comfortable with the choices they make about their child's health.

When parents take their baby in for regular checkups, they feel good because they know they're doing the most they can to keep their baby healthy and prevent him from getting sick.

As a home visitor, you can encourage parents to take their baby to their health care provider for regular checkups and immunizations. Discussing with parents ways to keep their baby healthy may be a good time to remind them to try to keep themselves healthy, too. By staying healthy themselves, parents will be able to take better care of their baby.

Preventing Illness

Germs are everywhere. They are in the air, on our hands, and in our mouths. We all are exposed to germs every day. Sometimes our bodies are healthy enough to fight off the germs and we don't get sick. Sometimes, if we are tired or just getting over another sickness, our bodies aren't able to fight the germs and we get sick. The same is true for babies.

When people get sick, they have a lot of germs that can be spread to others, which can make them sick, too. If someone has a cold and is coughing, the air around that person becomes filled with germs. Another person can breathe in that air and the germs and become ill. This is why people with colds should cover their mouths when they cough or sneeze. A person who is sick should also wash their hands before touching something another person will touch, especially food or dishes. Regular hand washing is a good way to keep from spreading germs.

Babies are exposed to germs every day. When parents take their baby to the store, to their health care provider's office, or to the homes of family members or friends, she comes in contact with a lot of germs. Sometimes the baby is healthy enough to stay well. At other times, the germs make her sick.

Parents can do many things to keep their baby strong and healthy so he is able to fight germs and not get sick. The best protection against germs is a healthy body. Babies stay healthy when they get enough food and the right kind of food, when they get enough sleep, and when they get love from family members. Parents can keep their baby healthy by keeping him clean, keeping the place where they live clean, keeping toys clean, and by trying to keep their baby away from people who are sick.

As a home visitor, you can encourage parents to keep themselves and their baby healthy. One thing you can do is try and set a healthy example to the parents whenever you can. Every so often, ask the parents if they are having any problems taking care of their health.

Hearing and Seeing (and Teeth, Too)

When babies are sick and have a fever, parents usually know something is wrong because their babies are hot and they act differently. When babies hurt themselves by falling, parents know something is wrong because the baby may have a cut or bruise. However, it isn't always easy for parents to know when something is wrong with their baby's hearing or sight.

When babies are born deaf or blind, parents and health care professionals usually know something is wrong because the babies do not react when there are things to hear or see. Total deafness and total blindness are usually noticed when babies are very young. Health professionals can work with parents to help their babies continue to grow and develop and to learn to live without their hearing or sight.

When a baby's sight or hearing isn't completely normal, it can be harder for the parents to know that something is wrong. Babies who have poor hearing may react when they hear loud noises, but they might be missing many softer sounds, such as talking. Babies who have poor sight will be able to follow bright lights with their eyes, but they might not be able to clearly see things that are either close or far away from them.

At regular checkups, most health care providers don't do a full test of a baby's hearing and sight unless they notice a problem. If the parents have watched their baby closely and think that he might have a hearing or seeing problem, they should tell their health professional and ask them to test their baby's hearing or sight.

Problems with the teeth or the mouth may be more difficult to see, but they can interfere with the development of talking or cause eating problems. Parents should ask their dentist about any problems they can see and at what age their baby should begin visiting the dentist.

As a home visitor, you can encourage parents to watch closely for hearing, sight, and teeth problems in their baby. If parents find out their baby has a hearing, sight, or tooth problem, help them find health professionals who can work with the family to develop a treatment plan. Early treatment makes a big difference, in most cases, to how well a baby grows and develops. Parents who learn as much as they can will help their baby, too.

How to Be Ready for Illness

We prepare for many things in life. We prepare for meals by shopping for food and cooking it. We prepare for sleep by putting on pajamas. We prepare for holidays and festivals by cooking special food, making special costumes, or decorating our homes or places of worship.

Parents need to prepare for illnesses in the family, too. It's a fact of life for parents that their baby will at some time get sick. Caring for a sick baby can be a very difficult task, especially if the parents aren't prepared to deal with an illness. With a few simple preparations for illnesses, parents can have the peace of mind of knowing that they will be ready for those times when their baby gets sick.

The parents you visit will have many questions and concerns when their baby becomes sick. As a home visitor, you can encourage the parents to do as much as they can to be prepared for illnesses.

There are several things parents can do to prepare for illnesses. The most important is for parents to **know how to get help**. If parents visit a particular health care provider's office regularly, they should know what its hours are and what phone numbers to use at what times of day.

At home, parents need to put important phone numbers where they can be found quickly. They need numbers for their health care provider, pharmacy, and family or friends who can help. Parents need to know where the office or clinic is and the best way to get there. Parents need to know how to take their baby's axillary (underarm) temperature to know if their baby has a fever. The health care provider's office or clinic will want to know this information.

These are very simple things, but they may be difficult for parents if they have a lot of stress in their lives, such as not having enough money, moving a lot, or living with many other people.

One of the most important things you can do as a home visitor is to help the parents be prepared for illnesses.

If parents are prepared for illnesses, can take an axillary temperature, and know how to tell when their baby has a fever, they will feel more confident in their abilities to care for their sick baby. They can take better care of their baby and will be less likely to go to the hospital emergency room each time their baby is sick.

When a Child is Sick

Most of the time, babies are healthy—they eat, sleep, and play as usual. When babies get sick, they may act differently than they usually do. They might cry more. They might stop eating. They might sleep more than usual or not be able to sleep at all. It may seem that, all of a sudden, many things about the baby are different.

Because parents love their babies so much, they get scared when their baby gets sick. They don't want their baby to hurt or have anything bad happen to him. A parent can get so worried that they take their baby to the hospital emergency room or call their health care provider in the middle of the night. If the situation is a true emergency, that is okay, but most of the time the baby isn't sick enough to need emergency care. Although it's hard to wait until the office or clinic opens, parents should try to help their baby at home until they can call the office or clinic and find out whether their baby needs to be examined by a health professional.

When their baby gets sick, parents may wonder if they did something wrong. Health professionals will ask the parents questions to find out more about the illness. Parents should not feel like they have done a bad job if they have done their best to keep their baby healthy. Sometimes, no matter how well parents take care of their baby, she will get sick. When their baby does get sick, parents need to focus their energy and attention on their baby, not on worrying about whether they have been bad parents.

Parents must learn how to give their baby medicine. It's very important that parents understand the right way to give medicine. They need to remember that it takes time for the medicine to make their baby feel better. A parent should not think that the medicine doesn't work or that the health professional has made a mistake if the baby doesn't get better right away. It can take a few days for a baby to begin feeling better. Practicing giving their baby medicine can make parents less worried, too, and able to concentrate on their baby's care, instead of their worry.

It's hard to take care of a sick baby. Parents usually sleep less. They may worry a lot. Parents may feel bad because their baby feels bad. They want their baby to feel better, but it can take a few days or even a week before their baby is healthy again.

While their baby is sick, parents need to take care of themselves, too. If they start feeling too tired, angry, or frustrated to handle their sick baby, they should ask someone to come over and help out. Your visit can be a good time for parents to talk about their feelings about taking care of their sick baby. You can let the parents know it's okay to feel tired and upset and that it's okay to get some help. Parents should try to take care of themselves when their baby is healthy, too. That way, when their baby does get sick, they will have the energy to take care of her.

Your role as a home visitor is to support parents when their baby gets sick. A call from you might be just what they need at the end of a hard day. Parents need someone to tell them that they're good parents, that their baby will get well again, and that an illness is only temporary.

Illness and Physical Problems

Over the first two years of life, most babies will have an average of eight occurrences of typical childhood illnesses, such as colds, ear infections, vomiting, or allergies, or physical problems, such as teething, diaper rash, or diarrhea. While these things may be a common and even expected part of being a parent, they can cause a lot of worry and stress for parents—especially new parents—when they do happen.

The parents will have questions and concerns when their baby gets sick. As a home visitor, you can provide the parents with information about the different illnesses and how to treat them. The visit can be a time for parents to share their feelings about their child's illnesses and to offer support to and receive support from each other, too.

Healthy Child/Sick Child's parent book has brief descriptions of some of the most common childhood illnesses and physical problems. The information in the book isn't intended to provide all that you or the parents will need to know about specific problems. Other resources, such as books, pamphlets, and health care workers, are good places to go for other important information about illnesses. The purpose of the parent book is to help the parents become familiar with some of the symptoms of common illnesses and physical problems and some methods for treating them.

Parents may be concerned about an illness or a problem at a specific time. For example, in the winter, they may be concerned about colds. When their baby gets older, they may want to learn about teething. When their baby starts eating solid foods, they might be interested in allergies. You may want to spend time in one visit quickly going over all the different illnesses and symptoms. Then, if their baby gets sick later, the parents will know where the information is. You can spend another visit, if necessary, on any specific illnesses.

In addition to knowing about these illnesses and problems, parents need to be sensitive to their baby's feelings when she's sick. It may help for parents to put themselves in their baby's position. You can help by reminding parents that babies have feelings, too, and the same things that parents feel when they're sick, babies will feel as well. For example, if the parents remember how sore their noses feel after they have wiped them over and over, they may be a little more patient when their baby pulls her face away from the tissue. If they remember how nice it felt when someone offered a little "tender loving care" when they were sick, they may be willing to hold their baby even when they want or need to be doing something else.

Concerns to Be Aware of During Home Visits

If you do notice any of these concerns, discuss them with the parents and/or your supervisor. Your supervisor will help you decide what needs to be done.

- Parents who do not take their baby in for regular checkups.
- A baby who does not seem to be healthy.
- Parents who think their baby doesn't need checkups or immunizations.
- Parents who don't trust anyone at their health care provider's office or clinic.

- Parents who have trouble keeping their baby's checkup appointments.

- A baby who is sick all the time.

- Parents who are sick all the time.

- Parents who don't try to keep their baby healthy.

- A baby with hearing problems.

- A baby with sight problems.

- Parents who know their baby has hearing or sight problems, but don't do anything about them.

- Parents who use the hospital emergency room for all medical care for their baby instead of a health care provider's office or clinic.

- Parents who don't have family, friends, or neighbors to call for help when they need it.

- Parents who don't have a way to get to their health care provider's office or clinic if their baby becomes sick.

- Parents who can't afford to buy basic medical supplies.

- Parents who can afford to buy basic medical supplies, but don't.

- Parents who don't call their health care provider when their baby is sick.

- Parents who panic and take their baby to the hospital emergency room every time he is sick.

- Parents who don't think it's important to give medicines the right way.

- Parents who get angry at their baby when he is sick.

- Parents who don't think it's important to know the signs of illnesses or problems.

- Parents who feel they don't need to do anything to help their baby feel better.

- Parents who never take their baby to their health care provider when she is sick.

Keeping Well

Checkups and Immunizations

Getting Ready

Agenda

- **Opening:** keeping your baby healthy
- **Keeping It Going:** checkups
- **Closing:** using what we've learned

Objectives

Parents will

- understand the importance of well-child checkups and immunizations
- learn what happens at a well-child checkup
- know the recommended immunizations schedule
- learn to prepare for their well-child checkup visit

In Advance

- Review the information in the parenting information book *Healthy Child/Sick Child.*

Materials

Activity 1: Why Checkups Are Important

- Young Family Parenting Information book *Healthy Child/Sick Child* for parents
- paper and pencil
- latest immunization schedule for your city or state
- latest information on vaccination side effects
- copy of an immunization record form

Getting Ready (continued)

Activity 2: Your Baby's Checkup—What Happens
- equipment, including a stethoscope, scale, tape measure, otoscope, thermometer, height/weight percentile chart (or contact your public health nurse for assistance)
- life-size baby doll
- paper and pencil

Activity 3: Talking with Your Health Care Professional
- several copies of the Checkup Questions (Part 1 and 2) form in Chapter 1 of the *Healthy Child/Sick Child* parent book

Checkups and Immunizations

If possible, find out who the family uses as a health care provider. It can help you provide more specific information.

Opening

"Regular medical checkups for our kids can reassure us that they are doing well and can find problems before they get too serious. Children grow best when they are healthy and checkups are part of taking good care of our children. We can get the most out of a doctor's visit if we are prepared with questions and concerns."

Keeping It Going

Activity 1: Why Checkups Are Important

Go over "How Will Checkups Help Your Child?" in Chapter 1. You can compare a checkup with preventative maintenance for cars or houses. It means recognizing and taking care of problems before they become serious.

Review the immunizations children need and the age when each shot is given.

- If the parents have their baby's immunization record, go over it to see if the child's immunizations are up-to-date. If they are, congratulate the parents on their attention to important health care.

- If the parents don't have an immunization record, help them start one using forms you may have brought or make one that includes the types of shot and date given.

- Parents need to maintain records of when their children get their immunizations. Proof of immunization is required for entering child care, preschool, and kindergarten.

- Encourage the parents to keep their child's health records in a safe, convenient place.

Both the type and frequency of recommended immunizations can change. Be sure to check with a doctor/clinic for the most recent recommendations.

There are parents who object to immunizations for religious or health reasons. Respect and listen to their concerns.

Use the latest information on vaccine side effects, how often kids in your community get the diseases, and other information from your local health department or other agency to answer the parents' questions and concerns about the immunizations.

Discuss the parents' concerns and the reasons to get children immunized.

Include in the discussion ways to help make their child more comfortable before, during, and after the immunizations.

Parents may have different reasons for not having gotten their child immunized. Some reservations may be

- concern about side effects of immunization
- doesn't know when or where to go to get shots
- cost
- religious reasons
- don't want to "hurt" their child
- parents' own fears

To many people, the disease names are just words. They may not know what the disease does. Use information from your health department to explain what these diseases are and how they affect children.

There can be side effects from the shots, but the protection the shots give outweighs the risk of side effects for most children. Most side effects are minor and the health professional will tell you how to deal with them.

Activity 2: Your Baby's Checkup—What Happens

Go over "What Happen at a Checkup" in Chapter 1 of the parent book.

Role play what happens at a well-child check with the doll. (Or, if the parents agree, you may involve their child.)

An older child may enjoy playing the "baby" in the doctor's visit.

Help the parents use a stethoscope and scale.

They can do other "doctor" things, too:

- measure their baby's head
- take their baby's temperature (see the "How to Be Ready for Illness" activity on how to take a baby's temperature)
- check their baby's ears with otoscope

If parents are concerned about their baby's height or weight, remind them to discuss this with their health care provider at the next checkup.

Ask the parents what information they received about their baby at previous doctor visits.

Discuss that information and use it to explain what might happen in other well-child visits.

Discuss some age-appropriate ways to make the well-child visit more comfortable for their child.
Making their baby comfortable during a well-child visit can help it go better for everyone. For example,

- Think about the time of day that would be good. Consider the parents' schedule, baby's schedule, transportation availability, and other variables.

- Hold the baby.

- Put the baby's blanket over the paper on the table.

- Be prepared with toys, snacks, and clean diapers.

- Even a well baby can be fussy during a doctor's visit. Being prepared can make it easier on everyone.

Ask the parents questions like these:

- How does your child react to unfamiliar people and surroundings?

- How do you think your child will react at the well-child visit?

- What can you do to help your baby feel more comfortable?

A parent's worries or fears can upset their baby and make the baby more anxious. Some things that might help:

- Parents shouldn't worry about their baby crying in the doctor's office. Health professionals are used to babies.

- Talk to the health professional about what will happen and how the parent feels.

Remind parents it is important to schedule health care visits in advance.
Help the parents make a form for planning regular appointments for well-child visits. Use the information in the parent book or from their health care provider on when visits should be scheduled. Be sure to include space to write the actual date and time of appointment.

Ask the parents if their baby's next visit has been scheduled. If so, fill in the date. If not, encourage the parents to call now and schedule it.

If parents use a drop-in clinic, discuss when a good time is to go and how to make waiting easier for parents and their child.

If parents are reluctant to call, do a role play on calling their health care provider to make an appointment.

In the role of appointment-taker, the home visitor should be sure to ask the parents questions about their baby's age, when they are available, etc. Discuss ways the parents can help make the call go smoothly.

- Know when you are available; check your calendar before you call.

- Have a calendar ready. Write the appointment down on your calendar.

- Be sure to go to the appointment or call and reschedule for another time if you can't make it.

After the role play, encourage the parents to call their health care provider to schedule the appointment.

Activity 3: Talking with Your Health Care Professional

Ask the parents to briefly share their last experience with their baby at the doctor.

Determine how that visit went and how they felt about the visit. You could ask these or similar questions:

- Did you remember to ask all your questions? Did you wish later you had asked something else?

- What was useful about the visit?

- What would you like to be different about the next visit?

Use the parents' comments about the visit—things they learned, what the doctor said—to reinforce the information parents can get at each visit.

Role play talking to clinic staff.

Some possible scenes

- Parents feel a lack of respect from the health care professional. Explore this with them and ask for specific examples or incidences. What are some options if this happens again?

- Parents feel too shy or be worried about asking "dumb" questions to get information they need.

Practice talking to helpful and unhelpful health professionals at a well-child check.

Help the parents realize that all parents have a right to know about their child's health. Parents can ask their health professional any questions they have about their children. Most health professionals want to help parents and their children. They may not realize that they appear too busy or intimidating. Urge the parents to be assertive in their need for information.

Brainstorm some ways to make it easier for parents to talk to their health care provider's staff.

Here are suggestions for the parents:

- Be prepared with the questions you want to ask or concerns you have.

- Be ready to give the health care provider information about your baby's day-to-day life.

- Practice asking questions in different ways.

- Keep asking your questions until you get the information you need.

Encourage the parents to respond fully to their health care professional's questions. One word answers are not helpful. Health care providers need the information parents can provide. They want to know that the parents understand and are involved in their child's health care, too.

Help the parents fill out the Checkup Questions (Parts 1 & 2) form in Chapter 1 of the parent book before going to a doctor's visit.

Show the parents how they can write down the questions that come up between visits.

Parents should also think about

- How will you react if the health professional gives you information you don't quite understand?

- How will you remember what the health professional says?

Leave a few blank copies of the form with the family to use for future visits.

Closing

Help parents summarize what they learned by going over these points. You may want to add others if you notice parents need more information.

- ✓ All children need regular medical checkups. There is a timetable of suggested ages for checkups. A regular checkup can find problems that parents can't see.

✓ Visits to the doctor can help the parents understand how their child will grow and develop and help them with problems with eating, discipline, or other issues.

✓ All children need to be immunized against childhood diseases.

✓ It is the parents' responsibility to schedule the checkups and to keep the appointments.

✓ Parents can make the most of their baby's checkups by being prepared with information about their baby and writing down their questions before going to the appointment .

✓ Parents can take advantage of the information the health professionals have by asking questions about their child's health and development.

Preventing Illness

Getting Ready _____

Agenda

- **Opening:** thinking about illness prevention
- **Keeping It Going:** hand washing to reduce germs
- **Closing:** using what we've learned

Objectives

Parents will

- learn how children get sick
- learn simple things they can do to keep their child from getting sick

In Advance

- Review the information in Chapter 1 in the parenting information book *Healthy Child/Sick Child.*

Materials

Activity 1: What Makes Kids Sick

- Young Family Parenting Information book *Healthy Child/ Sick Child* for parents
- paper and pencil
- magnifying glass

Getting Ready (continued)

Activity 2: Avoiding Illness—Daily Precautions

- soap
- bleach
- empty spray bottle
- one gallon bucket
- rubber gloves
- paper towels
- sink with water
- copy of the Wash Those Hands! handout at the end of this section

Preventing Illness

Opening

"All children get sick from time to time, usually when they have come in contact with germs. We can't avoid germs, but there are things we can do to help prevent illness."

Keeping It Going

Activity 1: What Makes Kids Sick

Talk about advice the parents have received about keeping their children well.

Parents get tons of advice on taking care of their kids to keep them from getting sick. Much of it may be information that really isn't true, but many people think it is. Share some of these tales. For example,

- Going outside with wet hair will give you a cold.

- Kids get sick as a punishment for something they've done or their parents have done.

What other advice or tales like these have the parents heard?

Review the information in Chapter 1 of the parent book on why children get sick. There are many reasons children get sick, but germs are the main reason. Germs are everywhere, but they are so tiny we can't see them without a microscope.

Be germ detectives.

Take a tour of the home with parents to discover all the places germs might hide. Continue the discussion about where to find germs. In general, they are everywhere! Use the magnifying glass to look closely at some areas. You can't see germs, but you can see where germs "hide":

- in the air and on the ground
- kitchens, bathrooms, bedrooms
- on towels, sponges, dish rags
- on toys, dishes, furniture, clothes
- around pets—fur, bowls, toys

Reassure the parents this isn't a housekeeping inspection. It's a chance to take a different look at their home and the places germs might be hiding. If parents are uncomfortable with a full tour, use only one or two rooms of their choice.

- baby's changing area
- on other people (ourselves, too!)—hands, mouths, hair…

Encourage the parents to think of places they might not usually cover when they are cleaning. Think of the cracks and crevices in the bathroom or kitchen, for example. Encourage the parents to pay special attention to these when cleaning house.

Brainstorm ways germs are spread:

- coughing, sneezing
- touching
- through shared items—telephones, cups, dishes…
- putting things in mouth—hands, pencils, toys…
- dishrags, unwashed counters, sinks, and similar things

So, do parents need to panic about germs and keep their families in a sealed atmosphere? Point out that even with all the germs around, people aren't sick all the time, but it is wise to take precautions to avoid germs.

Activity 2: Avoiding Illness—Daily Precautions

Review "Preventing Illness," Chapter 1 of the parent book, that lists good practices to maintain healthy families.
It is not possible to completely avoid germs, but we can do things to lessen the chances of getting sick.

Talk about any difficulties the parents might have. Help them think of some ways to improve the situation or make it easier.

Share information on how to keep germs from spreading.
Frequent hand washing is one good way to avoid germs. (See the Wash Those Hands! handout at the end of this section.)

Include these points:

- Soap has germ-killing properties. They come in bar and liquid form. All types of soap, not just those marked antibacterial have germ-killing properties.

Illnesses often pass from family member to family member. Encourage the parents to wash everybody's hands often, teach older kids to cover their mouths and noses when coughing and sneezing, not to share cups or toothbrushes, and to follow other precautions.

- Many soaps and cleaning products are labeled antibacterial. Some experts recommend that we limit use of antibacterial products because too much use can create germs that are resistant or difficult to kill.

If a sink is available, demonstrate hand washing.
Otherwise, just act it out. Follow the instructions on the handout on how to wash hands.

- A thorough hand washing takes about a minute. Suggest singing "Happy Birthday" while washing hands.

> Remind the parents to teach their child to wash his hands, too. If a child is 18 months or older, he can join in the demonstration.

Talk about keeping toys and other equipment clean.
Kids love to put toys and other stuff in their mouths. Washing and disinfecting toys and other equipment helps prevent the spread of germs.

Review the handout on how to clean and sanitize washable items.
Demonstrate how to make and use the cleaning solution.

- Make the solution according to the handout.
- Put some in a spray bottle for washing the high chair, etc.
- Wear rubber gloves when using bleach or other cleaning products.
- Clean some toys and equipment.

> Some products for antibacterial hand washing don't even need water. There are many brands, including Purell, Safeguard, and Softsoap. These products are on the store shelves next to the soap. Parents may want to keep a small bottle of one of these products in their diaper bag or purse for times when they must change diapers or use the restroom and no soap or water is available.

Closing

Help parents summarize what they learned by going over these points. You may want to add others if you notice parents need more information.

> Experts now recommend that we use fewer products marked "antibacterial" because overuse may cause germs to become resistant. All soap will kill germs.

✓ Germs cause many illnesses.
✓ Germs are everywhere people are. Germs are spread through contact with a person or object, through the air as with sneezing and coughing, and other ways.
✓ Frequent hand washing with soap can make a difference in our health.
✓ Keeping our houses clean, sanitizing our child's toys, and generally being aware of how to prevent illness will help keep our family healthy.

> Can houses be too clean? Recent research shows that children need some exposure to germs to develop immunities to common illnesses.

Hearing and Seeing (and Teeth, Too)

Agenda

- **Opening:** early attention to sight, hearing, and teeth
- **Keeping It Going:** what to look for
- **Closing:** using what we've learned

Objectives

Parents will

- understand the importance of checking a child's sight, hearing, and teeth

In Advance

- Review the information in the parenting information book *Healthy Child/Sick Child.*

Materials

Activity 1: Your Child's Hearing

- Young Family Parenting Information book *Feeding Your Child* for parents
- noisemakers like soft bells, music, box, rattle, or radio

Activity 2: Your Child's Sight

- brightly colored toys
- black and white toys or simple pictures or designs
- colored lights, like holiday lights
- object on a string
- gear your choices to the age of the child

Getting Ready (continued)

Activity 3: Your Child's Teeth

- diagram or model of toddlers' teeth
- up-to-date recommendations about toddler tooth care
- toddler-size toothbrush and toothpaste
- copy of the Healthy Teeth handout at the end of this section

Hearing and Seeing (and Teeth, Too)

Opening

"A baby's vision or hearing can change at any time. Observant parents can often spot a change earlier than a doctor can. Baby teeth need special care, too. Attention to a baby's vision, hearing, and teeth is important since early treatment can make a difference in how a condition can be treated."

Keeping It Going

Activity 1: Your Child's Hearing

Ask the parents about their own hearing.
Have they ever had an ear infection or a cold that affected their hearing? How did they feel without the full range of hearing?

Review "Your Child's Hearing" in the parenting information book on how a baby's hearing may be damaged.

Discuss with the parents whether their baby has had any of these possible causes of hearing loss.

Review what to look for when observing a baby's hearing. Encourage the parents to do these simple checks every so often, especially after the baby has had a cold or ear infection or a head injury. Hearing can change at any time.

Demonstrate these simple hearing checks.

- Sit behind the baby.

- Make a soft noise with the bell.

- Does the baby turn toward the noise? If yes, the baby's hearing is probably fine. If no, make slightly louder noises until the baby does turn toward the noise.

- Vary the types of noises to see if the baby reacts—deep noises like a gong and higher noises like bell or a sharp noise like hand clapping. Does she respond to the music box?

If the parents have any concerns about their baby's hearing, they need to call their health care provider to schedule a more complete hearing test.

Now encourage the parents to try these same checks with their baby. This can be a fun game for both parents and their baby.

Another way to see if a baby is hearing is to watch to see if she is "talking" to herself. Does she make noises—bubbling, cooing, trying to communicate with noises. Does she respond to her parents' voices and other familiar voices? Does she respond to a whispered voice? Does she like toys that make noise?

Activity 2: Your Child's Sight

Talk about the parents' vision.
Do they wear glasses or have any sight problems? Some conditions are inherited, some may develop later in life.

Discuss things that can affect a baby's sight.
Read to parents the list of things that might be problems from "Your Child's Sight" in the parenting information book. Are any of these conditions present? Encourage the parents to observe their baby's eyes and vision. They may be able to spot changes in their baby's sight. If any of these seem to be present, suggest that the parents call and schedule an appointment with their health care provider to discuss and test their baby's sight.

Demonstrate these simple vision checks.
Use the check appropriate for the baby's age.

Under 4 Months

- Lay the baby on floor or in an infant seat. Be sure you can see the baby's eyes.

- Take one toy and try to get the baby to notice it. Hold it about 12 inches from his face.

- When the baby notices the toy, move it slowly from one side of the baby's face to the other.

- Watch the baby's eyes. Does he seem to follow the toy with his eyes?

- Next, move the toy from the top of the baby's face to the bottom.

- Watch the baby's eyes. Does he seem to follow the toy with his eyes?

- Try this with different toys to see if the baby likes to look at one thing more than another.

Parents may have seen even tiny babies wearing glasses or eye patches. This means the parents and doctor have caught a problem early and by starting treatment young, may be able to correct the problem or prevent it from becoming worse. We may think, "that poor baby," but really it's a lucky baby to have such early attention.

Over 4 Months

- Follow same steps as above.

- Then choose one toy and tie an 8" to 10" string to it.

- Hold the toy up and try to get the baby to notice it. When he does, hold the toy on the string near the baby's face and see if he reaches for it. Watch the baby's eyes as he reaches for toy.

Point out that in addition to checking their baby's vision, these games are fun and encourage development. A mom or dad can play them anytime with their baby.

Encourage parents to do these checks every so often, especially if there are any changes with their baby's eyes or vision or any time any of the problems listed in the parent book happen.

Activity 3: Your Child's Teeth
Share the information your have about tooth development.
Use the diagrams/models to show which teeth usually come in first.

Here are some points to include:

- Baby teeth can appear as early as four months or even earlier. (Some babies are born with teeth!). Usually by age 3, a child will have all his baby teeth.

- Even though baby teeth aren't permanent, they must last a long time. Permanent teeth don't all grow in until a child is 13 or 14 years old.

- Teeth are vulnerable to decay from the beginning. Good tooth care is always important.

- A good diet helps prevent tooth decay. Sugar and carbohydrates (which break down into sugars) and sticky foods are the worst culprits. Cheese may actually help prevent cavities. How long food stays on teeth is more significant than how much is eaten. Check with your dentist about diet and tooth care and encourage your kids to brush or rinse after eating or drinking.

Find out whether or not your local water supply is fluoridated. Check to see if the family's water supply is filtered and if the filtered water no longer contains fluoride. Explain the decay prevention properties of fluoride to parents. Encourage parents to ask their dentist about fluoride if they have questions or concerns.

Demonstrate the proper toothbrushing technique.
Use the diagram/models or a cooperative child. Give the child the toothbrush and toothpaste. Some toddlers don't want any help when brushing their teeth. Brainstorm ways to make the process easier for parents and their child.

Here are some ideas to help parents care for their child's teeth:

- Make tooth brushing a game—"mistakenly" brush the child's nose, ear, whatever.

- Take turns brushing. Let your child brush your teeth, then you brush his.

- Let your child choose his own colorful toothbrushes.

- Let your child brush his own teeth first and then have the parent finish the job.

Give the parents the handout Healthy Teeth about tooth care.

Closing

Help parents summarize what they learned by going over these points. You may want to add others if you notice that parents need more information.

- ✓ A baby's hearing can be damaged by many things including ear infections, other illness, and injury.
- ✓ A baby's sight can be damaged by many things including eye infections, other illness, and injury.
- ✓ Regular, simple hearing and vision checks can identify problems early.
- ✓ Any concerns about a baby's hearing or sight should be immediately discussed with their health care provider.
- ✓ "Baby teeth" need special care, too. Encourage regular brushing and visiting a dentist if the parents notice any unusual signs. Regular dentist visits can begin when most baby teeth are in.
- ✓ Observant parents may spot a problem earlier than their health care provider would. Early detection is important because a sight or hearing impairment or a dental problem can interfere with a child's development in many ways.

Sick Child

Be Ready for Illness

Agenda

- **Opening:** all babies get sick
- **Keeping It Going:** helping your sick baby
- **Closing:** using what we've learned

Objectives

Parents will

- be prepared for their child's illness
- learn how to take their child's axillary (underarm) temperature

In Advance

- Review the information in the parenting information book *Health Child/Sick Child.*

Materials

Activity 1: What to Do Before Your Child Gets Sick

- Young Family Parenting Information book *Health Child/Sick Child* for parents
- supplies, medicine, and equipment listed in the Medicine and Supplies chart of the parenting information book
- paper and pencil

Activity 2: How to Take a Baby's Temperature

- humorous pictures or cartoons of a baby's reaction to getting his temperature taken
- different types of thermometers—digital, mercury, ear

Be Ready for Illness

Opening

"All babies will get sick at sometime or another. It can be scary for parents when their baby is sick, but by being prepared with information and supplies, they can deal with it more easily. Practice taking your baby's axillary temperature when she isn't sick. This will make it easier to do when it is necessary. It will also give the parents their baby's 'normal' temperature for comparison."

Keeping It Going

Activity 1: What to Do Before Your Child Gets Sick

Ask the parents how they prepare for an expected event, such as a holiday?
Do they have a checklist of things that must be done to get ready?

Point out that planning for an expected event makes sense—it makes it easier to have a list of what needs to be done and when. They can plan for unexpected events, like a child's illness, too. Discuss with the parents how to prepare for something unexpected—since they don't know exactly what will happen, how can they know what needs to be done?

Lead the parents through a discussion of how they can be prepared for when their child gets sick. Review the ideas in the parent book.
Brainstorm a list of all the numbers/addresses parents need to know when their child is sick. Include the after-hours clinic, pharmacy, and taxi phone numbers. List the hours they are open and other important information. Discuss a good, safe place to keep the list, such as on a bulletin board or on the refrigerator.

Remind parents they may not need to take their child to the doctor every time he's sick.
Sometimes a health care provider can tell us what to do over the phone. In the parent book, there is a list of some items to have on hand for when their baby is sick. Discuss each item on the list to see if the parents are familiar with what each one does.

Encourage parents to ask their health care provider for some guidelines about when to call.

Go over the items you brought and any others on the list. Ask the parents if they have the item or any questions about what it is or how to use it. Make a list of the items the parents don't have. You may be able to help them think of ways to get the items—ask the clinic for medicine samples, for example.

Activity 2: How to Take a Baby's Temperature

Show the parents the cartoons.
Talk about what the baby is "thinking" about when having her temperature taken. Point out the other ways to take a temperature besides rectally. In fact, parents should **only** take their baby's axillary temperature, that is, her underarm temperature.

Parents should not take their baby's temperature rectally. Leave that to the clinic. Show parents how to take an axillary (underarm) temperature.

Work with the parents to practice taking their baby's temperature when the baby feels good.
Use an easy-to-read thermometer. Go over the instructions on taking a baby's axillary temperature. If they agree, help the parents take their baby's temperature right now.

Many parents are hesitant to take their baby's temperature because they are not sure how to do it, but it is important to be able to report the baby's temperature when they call the doctor when she's sick. Help the parents make a note of their baby's healthy, normal temperature so they will know when their baby has a fever or a below normal temperature.

Mercury thermometers can be hard to read accurately. If parents seem to be having trouble reading a mercury thermometer, suggest they purchase an inexpensive digital thermometer. This type gives the readout in a display screen on the thermometer. Some even beep when ready to be read.

Remind the parents to tell their health care provider that the temperature they're reporting is the axillary temperature.
An axillary temperature will be different than one taken orally. The health care provider needs accurate information to make recommendations.

Closing

Help parents summarize what they learned by going over these points. You may want to add others if you notice parents need more information.

- ✓ All babies get sick at some time (and it may seem like it's always at night!).
- ✓ Parents can prepare ahead of time for when their baby is sick so they are ready to help their sick baby.

✓ Parents need to know how to get help when their baby is sick, including knowing important phone numbers, where to go for help, and how to get there.

✓ Parents need to know when their baby has a temperature. Having a thermometer on hand and knowing how to take their baby's axillary (underarm) temperature is an important part of being prepared for their child's illness.

When a Child Is Sick

Agenda

- **Opening:** how to know if your baby is sick
- **Keeping It Going:** what to do when your baby is sick
- **Closing:** using what we've learned

Objectives

Parents will

- recognize symptoms of illness
- know when to call their health care provider and what to say
- practice giving their baby medicine
- learn ways to help both baby and parents feel better when their baby is sick

In Advance

- Review the information in Chapter 2 of the parenting information book *Healthy Child/Sick Child.*

Materials

Activity 1: How to Know If Your Child Is Sick

- Young Family Parenting Information book *Healthy Child/Sick Child* for parents
- paper and pencil

Activity 2: When to Call the Doctor and What to Say

- Write on index cards the reasons to call a health care provider's office or clinic. (Use the parenting information book.)
- Write on index cards the reasons not to call a health care provider's office or clinic.
  - baby has an axillary temperature of 99° F
  - baby vomits once after a meal

Getting Ready (continued)

> - baby has diarrhea in one diaper
> - child will not eat lunch one day
> - child has a runny nose for three days
> - child has a cough for two days
> - child gets a finger caught in the door; finger is bruised
> - child has rash on stomach for one day
> - child falls down on sidewalk; hand is scraped
> - child gets a sunburned face

- toy or real telephone
- extra copies of the form in the parent book for recording information to give the health care provider
- phone stickers that list emergency numbers, including the Poison Control Center
- blank stickers for parents to put their own phone number and address on for their phone

Activity 3: How to Give Medicine to Babies

- different types of medicine dispensers—syringes, dropper, measuring spoons, little measuring cups that come with some medicines
- water or formula to use as medicine
- prescription bottle with label
- over-the-counter medicine with bottle and label such as children's Tylenol

When a Child Is Sick

Opening

"Changes in normal behavior, especially more than one change, can often indicate that a child is sick. When your baby is sick, you can take care of her and help her feel better if you are prepared: know how to take your baby's axilllary temperature, know when to call your health care provider, and know how to give your baby medicine."

Keeping It Going

Activity 1: How to Know If Your Child Is Sick

Ask the parents if they know when they are getting sick? How do they know?
A baby can't say that he doesn't feel well, so parents must be able to recognize when their baby isn't well.

Go over the information on the signs of a sick child in the parenting information book. Ask the parents to describe a normal day with their baby. You can take some notes if that helps the parents.

Here are some questions to ask the parents:

- What time does your baby usually wake up?
- Is he usually cheerful when he wakes up?
- How much does he usually eat?
- Does he nap?
- What does he like to do during the day?

Continue the conversation so the parents get a picture of how their baby behaves when he is well. Then ask

- How do you think his behavior might change if he were sick?

Review the signs of illness.
You may want to discuss other things that might cause a change in their baby's behavior, but wouldn't necassarily mean their baby is sick. For example, teething can cause fussy behavior, but teething isn't being sick.

You can discuss ways to comfort a teething baby or other fussy baby.

Remind parents that if their baby's normal behavior changes, it can be a sign of illness, but it can also be a sign of development and growth. Parents need more than one piece of information to decide if their baby is sick.

Activity 2: When to Call the Doctor and What to Say

Ask the parents to think about the last time they were sick.
Did they call their health care provider or just treat themselves at home? How did they decide what to do? With a sick child, how do the parents know when to call their health care provider and when to treat a minor illness at home? Discuss some recent times when either the parents or their baby were sick.

Play the game.
Put the index cards in a bowl or bag. Have the parents take turns picking a card, reading the description, and then deciding if there is a reason to call their health care provider. Discuss these situations and others that could happen and whether or not a parent should call their health care provider.

Ask some questions like these:

- In this case, would you call immediately or could you wait until morning?

- Have you asked your health care provider about when you should call?

- What if you really don't know what to do—should you call?

- Does your health care provider have a number to call just for information questions?

Briefly go over the reasons to call their health care provider during regular office hours. Reassure the parents that it is important to call at night or on weekends if their child is really sick. Remind the parents to have the after-hours number for their health care provider handy for when they need it.

Act out a telephone conversation.
Decide on an "illness" for the child. It could be one of the things described in the above activity or a recent illness of the child. Review the information in the parenting information book that lists information their health care provider may want to know.

Act out a telephone conversation about the child's illness with the health care provider . The home visitor can act as the clinic staff person and ask a variety of questions about the child's current condition—temperature, length of illness if it's gotten worse, vomiting, diarrhea, and other questions.

Show the parents how to use the forms in the parent book to record the information to have at hand when calling their health care provider. Leave the extra copies of the forms for future use.

Help the parents determine when a situation is a true emergency.
These are some emergencies:

- ✓ child is having problems breathing; is turning blue or choking
- ✓ bleeding that cannot be controlled
- ✓ child is unconscious or unresponsive, evenly briefly
- ✓ child has swallowed poison or non-food substance

In an emergency, call 911 or the local emergency number. In case of poisoning, call Poison Control Center. They will tell you what to do.

You may want to talk about teaching older children when and how to call 911, too.

Role play making an emergency call to 911 or the Poison Control Center.
In an emergency, anyone can be flustered or confused.

When calling, a dispatcher will ask

- your name and address
- baby's age
- the condition
- Poison Control will ask what the baby ate; have the box or bottle with you when you call

Help the parents put stickers on all phones so important emergency numbers are always at hand.
Suggest that parents keep a sticker on their phones with their address and phone number on it, too. It may seem odd to do so, but it is very easy for parents to temporarily forget even the most obvious things during an emergency. It also helps babysitters and others who may need to call and might not know the address.

Activity 3: How to Give Medicine to Babies

Review the guidelines for giving medicine.
Remind the parents that part of giving medicine is giving the right dose. Too much or too little may make medicine not work.

Go over the prescription bottle's label with the instructions.
Be sure to point out this information:

- dosage instructions (amount to give)
- where to give medicine—by mouth, in ears
- how often to give medicine
- length of time to give medicine
- other instruction labels on bottle—take with food, finish all medicine, stay out of sunlight, keep medicine refrigerated
- number of refills

Repeat with the over-the-counter medicine label. Go over the label and dosage information together. Remind the parents not to give any medicine to their child unless their health care provider has instructed them to.

Remind the parents of the importance of giving the right dose.
Too much medicine can make a child sick; too little won't help him get well. It is important to finish any prescription medicine, too, even if the baby seems to feel better after a few days. If the child is younger than six months old, parents may need to call their health care provider to find out how much over-the-counter medicine to give. This is usually indicated on the label.

Show parents the different types of medicine dispensers.

- Look at different medicine dispensers; discuss the pros and cons of each type.
- Show the parents how to read the dosage on the different medicine dispensers.
- Look at the prescription bottle for the prescribed dose.
- Ask the parents to measure out this dose using water or formula.

Tell parents that medicine should not be put in their baby's food or formula. The baby may not finish the food or bottle and would not get the right dose of medicine.

Giving medicine to a baby can be a challenge. Sometimes finding the right medicine dispenser can make a difference. Which types have the parents used? How did they work?

If it is okay with the parents, have them practice giving their baby "medicine." Use water or formula as "medicine"—with the different types of dispensers.

Watch the baby and see how she reacts to each type. Did one work better than another?

Closing

Help parents summarize what they learned by going over these points. You may want to add others if you notice parents need more information.

✓ Babies cannot tell parents if they are sick. Parents can watch for changes in their baby's behavior to know when she might be sick.

✓ Be prepared with a detailed description of your child's symptoms before calling your health care provider. This will help the parents remain calm and focused when they call.

✓ Parents need to know how to read and interpret the information on prescription and over-the-counter medicine labels. Always follow the instructions exactly.

Remind parents that, even though we are using the water or formula in place of medicine, they should never call medicine "candy" to try to get their child to take it. This may encourage their child try to take the medicine when she shouldn't.

Caring for Sick Child

Agenda

- **Opening:** knowing when your baby is sick
- **Keeping It Going:** helping your baby feel better
- **Closing:** using what we've learned

Objectives

Parents will

- recognize symptoms of common childhood illnesses
- learn how to care for a sick child with a common illness

In Advance

- Review the information in Chapter 3 of the parenting information book *Healthy Child/Sick Child.*

Materials

Activity 1: How Does a Sick Baby Feel?

- Young Family Parenting Information book *Healthy Child/ Sick Child* for parents
- Using information in the parenting information book, make a deck of game cards with one illness sympton per card.

Activity 2: Taking Care of a Sick Child

- Using information in the parenting information book, make cards listing one illness or condition per card. Include one card for each common illness, too, as a reminder of what they are.
- Make another deck of cards listing ways to help a baby feel better.

Caring for Sick Child

Opening

"Parents can learn to recognize symptoms of common illnesses and learn ways to make their babies feel better. No matter what the illness, your baby will need a lot of extra love and attention when he feels sick."

Keeping It Going

Activity 1: How Does a Sick Baby Feel?

Remind the parents that almost every baby and child will get sick at some time or another.
Common illnesses for babies and children include colds, ear infections, vomiting, diarrhea, and diaper rash. Some babies will have discomfort when teething. Some may be allergic to different things like some foods, dust, or pollen from plants. Ask the parents if their child has experienced any common illness or allergy.

Review the list of symptoms of different illnesses.
Go over each one with the parents and point out that some of the symptoms are similar for various illnesses.

Play the game.
The cards have descriptions of symptoms of illnesses or conditions of babies. Take turns picking a card, reading the description, and then deciding what it might mean if baby has that symptom. If parents can't decide what it might be from the first card, take another card and continue on until the parents can make a "diagnosis" of what the illness might be. Point out that parents must look at all the "evidence" before deciding what their baby might have.

Ask some questions like these:

- Has your baby ever shown symptoms like these?
- What have you done about it when you've noticed symptoms?

Activity 2: Taking Care of a Sick Child

Go over the recommendations on how to make a sick baby or child feel better.

There is more information about this in Meld's Young Family Parenting Information book *Healthy Child/Sick Child.* You may want to review this information or use it as part of this visit, too.

Point out the recommendations for when to call your health care provider.

Remind the parents that all sick babies need a lot of extra love and attention when they are sick.
Special cuddling and soothing can help a baby better cope with being sick.

Play the game.
Lay out the "illness" cards face up in a row. Place the "care suggestion" cards in a pile, face down. Have the parents draw a card and read the suggestion out loud. Then put the suggestion on the appropriate illness or condition. Discuss with the parents the many ways they can help their child feel better, including holding and cuddling her.

Continue by discussing the frustration parents might feel when their child is sick. It can be hard to comfort a sick child, but parents will learn what makes their baby feel better.

You may want to go over the specifics of what to do for an illness if the child happens to be sick during your visit.
It may be a good idea, too, to review some of the recommendations in detail. For example, you may want to talk about what "clear liquids" means and when and how to give them or review the recommendations for diarrhea.

You know the parents and how much information they may need or want. Since this activity may not be something they can use right now, you can go over it quickly now and then come back to it when their baby is sick.

Closing

Help parents summarize what they learned by going over these points. You may want to add others if you notice parents need more information.

- ✓ Parents can learn the signs of illnesses and other problems and look for these signs when they think their baby might be sick.
- ✓ There are ways parents can help their sick baby feel better.
- ✓ Parents need to give their baby a lot of love and attention when their baby isn't feeling well.
- ✓ Parents can learn what they can do at home to help their sick baby and when they should call their health care provider for help.

Handout

Wash Those Hands!

Steps to Help Stop the Spread of Germs

Hand washing is the single most important way to prevent the spread of germs. Here are steps followed in child care centers, schools, and medical clinics. They can be used at home to prevent the spread of common illnesses like colds and some diseases.

1. How to wash your hands

- Wet hands under warm, running water.
- Rub your hands together for at least 20 seconds using warm water and, preferably, liquid soap.
- Wash under fingernails, between fingers, back of hands, and wrists.
- Rinse your hands well under running water.
- Dry your hands with a paper towel.
- Turn off water using a paper towel instead of bare hands.

2. When to wash your hands

- before touching an infant/child
- before you prepare or serve food or set the table
- before you eat or drink
- after you use the bathroom or help a child use the bathroom
- after you change a diaper
- after you handle items soiled with body fluids or waste such as blood, drool, urine, stool, or discharge from nose or eyes
- after you clean up messes (blood, vomit, urine, or stool)
- after you have handled a sick child

3. When to wash your child's hands

- after he uses the bathroom
- after she has touched a child or infant who has been sick
- after he has played outside
- before and after playing with moist items such as play dough
- before and after she eats

4. Items to be cleaned and sanitized

Use a solution made by adding one tablespoon of bleach to one gallon of water. Put smaller items in this solution to clean and soak for a few minutes. Spray larger items with the solution (cribs, etc.). Do not rinse. Allow objects to air dry.

- toys and equipment (e.g., crib bars, walkers) — weekly or when soiled
- toys and objects that end up in baby's mouth — daily or when soiled
- high chair trays — after each use
- table tops — before and after eating
- crib mattresses — weekly or when soiled

Healthy Teeth

Good dental care begins early. Here are some suggestions
to help parents get started. Ask your health care provider or dentist
if they have other information about dental care for your baby.

Home Care

- Don't put your baby to bed with a bottle. If he falls asleep with a bottle, the juice or milk can pool against his teeth. This will cause tooth decay.

- Even before teeth appear, gently clean gums with a brush or wipe with finger wrapped in gauze or soft washcloth.

- Once teeth appear, help your child get into the habit of brushing in the morning, after lunch, and at night.

- Use a toothbrush designed for children— one with a small head and soft bristles. Replace every three months or when bristles look worn.

- Skip toothpaste until your toddler can rinse and spit out leftover toothpaste and foam. It's the "elbow grease"—the brushing—that actually cleans the teeth.

- Beware of fluoridated toothpaste and mouth rinses with young children. While fluoride is important, too much fluoride can actually damage teeth. Ask your dentist about using fluoride toothpaste or mouth rinses with your child.

- Brush teeth with a gentle back and forth motion across chewing surfaces; use a circular motion along the sides and the gum line; back and forth on inner surfaces, if you can. Gently brush gums where teeth haven't yet appeared.

- Let your toddler brush her own teeth when she shows an interest, but you will need to finish the job until she is around 7 years old.

- Teach him to rinse and spit so all bits of food are gone. Each family member should have his own cup for rinsing. And, of course, their own toothbrush!

Professional Care

- Recommendations vary as to when a child should first visit a dentist. Some say between six months and a year. Others say at age 3. When you decide to schedule the first visit depends on the condition of your toddler's teeth, your healthcare provider's advice, and your judgment.

- Any signs of abnormality—an open or unaligned or "bad" bite, dark spots or uneven coloration on the teeth— require attention.

- Injury to mouth or teeth should be seen by the dentist, too. Early attention to dental problems can prevent tooth decay and any mouth irregularities that might interfere with speech development.

- Try to choose a pediatric or children's dentist. They have training in treatment of children, are familiar with children's special needs, and are better prepared to handle the fears, restlessness, and questions of kids.

- Once teeth are in, a professional cleaning every six months will help prevent decay.

Chapter 4
Safe Child & Emergencies

Accidents

When Accidents Happen

Introduction

Home Visitor Information

The emphasis in this book is on prevention of accidents and keeping children safe in many situations. Parents can do a lot to make their homes and other areas safe for their baby and, since babies and young children cannot keep themselves safe, it is up to parents and other adults to watch out for them.

Understanding why accidents happen helps parents see their home and activities in a different way. Instead of going about their daily activities as they did before their baby arrived, you can help them see things that might be hazardous or cause an accident. Parents can then figure out ways to make the environment safer. Childproofing the home is one important way to help children avoid accidents, too. It is also important so their baby can explore his surroundings safely. Exploration is how babies learn about the world.

Even the most protected child with the most careful parents may have an accident. Help parents understand what to do in an accident and to be prepared to call the emergency services when necessary.

After the activities in *Safe Child & Emergencies*, parents will

- understand that it is up to them to prevent accidents because babies cannot keep themselves safe

- understand how a child's development affects what parents do to keep their baby safe

- learn how to childproof their homes and other areas to help keep their baby safe from accidents

- be aware of safety equipment and how to use it

- know the qualities of a good babysitter

- learn how to childproof the home

- be prepared in case of an accident

- know first aid for simple injuries

Important Information for Home Visitors

- Children cannot keep themselves safe. It's the parents' responsibility to do their best to prevent accidents from happening. Many accidents can be prevented.

- Young children **cannot** be left alone. Parents need to check on their baby again and again. Parents need to watch what their baby is doing and always remember to childproof their baby's environment.

- Accidents can happen when parents are busy. Well-rested and relaxed parents help make their children safer and happier.

- When a child has an accident, parents can help by staying calm, knowing basic first aid, and having emergency phone numbers nearby.

- All parents need to know about first aid—steps to take and basic supplies to have on hand. An illustrated, simple first-aid book for the home is also very helpful.

Additional Topic Information

Why Accidents Happen

Every year, more children die from accidents than from being sick. Parents can prevent many accidents, but to prevent accidents they have to know how and why accidents happen. Time of day can be a factor in accidents, as can parents' stress level. Other accidents are the result of unsafe conditions, parents' distractions, and other situations.

Many things can cause accidents. As babies develop and explore new things, accidents can happen. When a baby begins to crawl, she can get into many new situations. She may put their fingers into electrical outlets. She could find things on the floor and put them in her mouth. When a child is learning to walk, he can fall and hit his head. He may fall down the stairs. Babies want to try new things, but they can't always do them right away. Understanding how children develop will help parents anticipate what their baby might try next.

When parents are busy, accidents can happen. Stressed and distracted parents are thinking of other things, not their baby. Parents who can slow down and relax are better able to see things that might cause an accident. This will help them prevent accidents.

Sometimes parents leave their baby alone while they do other things, like washing clothes, going to the store, talking on the phone, or visiting with friends. When a baby is unsupervised, he may have an accident. Parents must understand that babies cannot keep themselves safe. It's up to parents and other adults to make a baby's environment a safe place and to always know where their baby is and what he is doing.

Stopping Accidents

As the first step to keeping their baby safe, parents need to

- know what their baby will be able to do in the next few months

- see danger for the baby by looking for things that might cause accidents

- change things at home so that accidents will not happen

Knowing these things can help parents be prepared to prevent accidents. By understanding child development, parents will be able to anticipate the next stage. If a baby is just starting to crawl, parents will know that pulling herself to standing might be next. They can look around and see what needs to change in the environment to keep their baby safe.

Childproofing a home helps prevent accidents. Parents can do these things and more to make the home safe for their baby:

- Put things up on shelves so the baby can't reach them.

- Keep their baby away from dangerous things like electrical outlets, stairs, the stove, or hot steam radiators by using safety devices, gates, or other methods.

These are just a few things parents can do. You and the parents will figure out many more during your visit.

Parents may have friends or family members who don't agree with childproofing. They may think that children should learn the word "no" and to be obedient. Help parents make decisions about what is best for their child by helping them understand child development so they know at what stage a child can understand "no" and control her urge to touch.

Keeping a child safe and childproofing a home and car are the best ways to prevent accidents, but not all accidents can be prevented. When accidents do happen, parents need to

- act quickly
- know how to take care of minor injuries and emergencies
- know how to give first aid
- know how and when to get medical help

When a child is hurt, parents often feel like they are to blame. They may feel guilty or worry others will blame them. Sometimes the guilt can keep parents from acting quickly. Parents can avoid feelings of guilt by keeping their baby safe, childproofing their home and car, and learning basic first aid. But, if an accident happens, parents should first think about getting help for the child. Parents need to **act quickly** and get their child medical help. After the emergency is over, they can then think about how to prevent the same accident in the future.

During and after an emergency, parents need to understand their feelings and try to remain calm and steady. You can help parents remain calm and do the right thing in an accident by going over how to treat minor injuries and practicing calls for medical help. Parents who are prepared are more likely to respond quickly and without fear. Parents will have confidence in their abilities after these visits.

Concerns to Be Aware of During Home Visits

If you do notice any of these concerns, discuss them with the parents and/or your supervisor. Your supervisor will help you decide what needs to be done.

- A child who seems to have many injuries and accidents.
- Parents who leave their baby alone and think it's okay.
- Parents who don't try to make their home or their car safe for their baby.
- Parents who don't watch their child carefully.
- Parents who don't childproof their homes because they don't know how or because they don't want to.
- Unsafe equipment that parents are using with their baby.

- Situations that parents talk about that might cause an accident.
- Parents who don't think it's important to learn first aid.
- Parents who seem afraid to call for medical help.

Accidents

Why Accidents Happen

Getting Ready _____

Agenda

- **Opening:** growing children may have accidents
- **Keeping It Going:** preventing accidents
- **Closing:** using what we've learned

Objectives

Parents will

- understand that it is up to them to prevent accidents because babies cannot keep themselves safe
- discuss how a child's development affects what parents do to keep their baby safe
- learn how to childproof their homes and other areas to help keep their baby safe from accidents

In Advance

- Review the information in the parenting information book *Safe Child & Emergencies.*

Materials

Activity 1: Why Accidents Happen

- Young Family Parenting Information book *Safe Child & Emergencies* for parents
- photos of the baby and parents you are visiting
- pictures of rooms like the bathroom and kitchen and household objects like razor, cleaning products, pill bottle, blinds with a cord, knife or scissors, stove, electrical appliances, bucket, lighted candle—any common object that could be part of an accident
- copy of the "Be Ready for Your Baby's Changes" chart in the parenting information book

Getting Ready (continued)

Activity 2: The Most Dangerous Times

- TV or radio
- deck of playing cards

Why Accidents Happen

Opening

"Accidents can hurt our children, but parents can prevent many accidents by being aware and being there. There is no substitute in accident prevention than the parents knowing the area and the situation, including how they and their child feel, the time of day, and always being alert to where their child is and what she is doing."

Keeping It Going

Activity 1: Why Accidents Happen

Begin by going over why accidents happen.

Accidents happen because babies and young children are eager to try new things. This is good, but babies have yet to develop the motor skills or knowledge to keep up with everything they want to do or try. Babies can't foresee what might happen and they can't remember what parents tell them, either. It is up to parents and other adults to watch out for their baby. Babies can't keep themselves safe!

Continue by telling the parents that accidents happen to many children every year. Explain that you aren't saying this to scare parents, but to help them think about how to prevent accidents to their baby.

The parents may know of a child who was badly hurt or even killed by an accident in the home or another place. Discuss some things that might have led up to the accident and what could have been done to prevent it.

Point out that several things must be present for an "accident" to happen.

These are

- a dangerous object or substance like a bottle of pills, a bucket of water, a staircase, etc.

- a person such as an unsuspecting toddler

- environmental conditions such as no childproof lid on the pills, water in the bucket, no gate on the stairs, etc.

- in accidents involving children, an adult not paying enough attention to the situation

Accidents can happen when a child is left in the care of a sibling who is not old enough or capable of caring for a young child. Talk about who parents can leave their children with so they can be sure they are safe.

Use the pictures and imaginary situations if parents are uncomfortable or threatened by using their home in this game.

Be understanding and nonjudgmental when pointing out potential accidents. Parents don't want to feel they have created a "house of hazards" for their children.

Another danger is younger siblings trying to keep up with older siblings. Remind parents to be aware of where each child is and what each is doing.

Point out that to prevent accidents and injury, parents must make change.
Parents can remove the dangerous object, teach their children good safety habits (depending on their age and ability to understand), and change the situation. Most of all, parents can be ever watchful over their children and make sure that any other adults who care for them are as watchful.

Play the game.
With the parents, survey the room you are in and find a situation that could lead to an accident. Or you can use the pictures and create situations. Use the baby picture and the parents' pictures in every situation. For example, put out a picture of a toilet with the lid up. Add the baby picture. Then ask, "What might happen?" (Baby could fall in toilet and drown.) Ask, "What could we change about the situation?" (Keep lid down and lock it with an appropriate safety latch; keep the bathroom door closed.) Add the parents' pictures to the group and ask, "What can parents do?" (Teach their baby not to play in bathroom; redirect their baby every time he heads to bathroom.)

Continue the game with other pictures or situations.
Then take a walk around the home and look for accidents that could happen. Put the baby picture near the situation and ask parents to describe an accident that might happen and how to prevent it. Remind the parents that the key to accident prevention is to be aware of what's going on around them and their children and being there to watch their kids and keep them safe.

Point out that as their baby grows, so does the possibility of an accident.
Babies are eager to try out new things. This eagerness can lead them into trouble if parents aren't aware of changes taking place. Children imitate their parents, too, and want to do what they do, like cook or go upstairs, but it may not be safe for them to do so. Parents need to be alert to what their baby is doing.

Use the "Be Ready for Your Baby's Changes" chart from the parenting information book to record how accidents might happen and how the parents can make their home a safe place for their child.

Help parents consider what accidents might happen at their child's current stage of development and how they can make their home safer to prevent accidents.

Use the cards or situations again, but this time ask what might happen at the next stage of development for their baby.

For example, if their baby is in the crawling stage now, what might happen in this situation when she learns to pull herself up and when she learns to walk. What can the parents do then to prevent accidents?

Activity 2: The Most Dangerous Times

Remind parents that accidents can happen when families are tired, busy, sick, overworked, or during other times of stress.

These conditions often mean parents are too tired or too busy to play close attention to the situation and their child. This inattention can lead to an accident.

Turn on the radio and/or TV.

Turn up the volume. Then take the deck of cards, one card at time, and ask the parents to try to build a house of cards. Give each card a characteristic of a bad situation. These could be things like—it's 5 p.m., mom is running late, the baby is hungry, siblings are squabbling over a toy, neighbors are fighting loudly, and so on. You can use some examples from the parenting information book.

Drugs, medication, and alcohol use can dull senses and make parents unaware of what's going on with their kids, too. Encourage parents to avoid drugs and alcohol and to be extra alert when on medication.

Ask the parents to predict how long it will be until the house of cards collapses under the distractions of the TV/radio, the struggle to get dinner, and all the other stuff going on.

Use this as an example of how certain times of the day or month can contribute to more accidents. Things can build and build and then collapse.

Discuss what to do about times when parents are stressed, distracted, or otherwise preoccupied so they have a chance to see the changes they can make to prevent accidents.

You can include the relaxation techniques and ways to slow down. Which of these techniques works best for each parent?

Closing

Help parents summarize what they learned by going over these points. You may want to add others if you notice parents need more information.

✓ Babies and children cannot keep themselves safe.

✓ As children grow and change, the possibility of an accident increases unless parents are aware of how their child has changed and what they can do to reduce the possibility of accidents.

✓ Accidents happen more often when families are tired, distracted, sick, busy, or too involved in daily activities to pay close attention to their child.

✓ We can learn ways to relax and slow down, which can help prevent accidents by giving us time and energy to pay attention to what's going on.

Stopping Accidents

Getting Ready

Agenda

- **Opening:** preparing for when accidents happen
- **Keeping It Going:** avoiding accidents
- **Closing:** using what we've learned

Objectives

Parents will

- discuss safety equipment and demonstrate how to use it
- look at the qualities of a good babysitter
- learn how to childproof the home

In Advance

- Review the information in the parenting information book *Safe Child & Emergencies*.

Materials

Activity 1: Being Prepared: Important Phone Numbers and Safety Equipment

- Young Family Parenting Information book *Safe Child & Emergencies* for parents
- copy of the "Preventing Accidents" form in the parent book to list emergency numbers
- phone stickers with emergency numbers, including the Poison Control Center
- safety equipment such as outlet covers, cupboard locks, door locks/hooks, toilet locks, smoke alarm, baby gate, carbon monoxide detector, and fire extinguisher
- common house materials that can be used instead of commercial items, such as duct tape to cover outlets or baking soda to extinguish small fires
- safety equipment you can give the parents to use in their home

Getting Ready (continued)

Activity 2: Helping Babysitters Be Responsible
- several copies of Ready to Go and the Babysitters Checklist handouts at the back of this section

Activity 3: Childproofing Home, Car, and Baby's Area
- safety equipment to install
- crayon or candle and paper cup (to use if the day is hot and parents have a car)

Stopping Accidents

Opening

"Parents can prevent many accidents by being prepared. This includes knowing who to call for help and when to call, choosing safe and responsible adults to care for our kids, and by doing a thorough job of childproofing our homes and other areas our children visit. Teaching our children about safety is part of helping them stay safe, too."

Keeping It Going

Activity 1: Being Prepared: Important Phone Numbers and Safety Equipment

Remind parents that being prepared to respond quickly if an accident does occur can make a difference in how seriously their child is hurt.

Review the numbers to call for various types of emergencies. Help the parents fill in the emergency numbers on the "Preventing Accidents" form numbers and decide where to post it. Help the parents put stickers on all their phones so important emergency numbers are always at hand.

Point out that another way to be prepared is to prevent an accident by using safety equipment available for homes.

Review the chart listing safety equipment in the parenting information book. Show the parents the examples you brought and demonstrate how to use them.

Take a tour of the home so parents can show you what they have done to child-proof.

Help the parents see where additional safety devices would be good and what type would work or not work. Install any devices that you brought to leave with the parents.

Activity 2: Helping Babysitters Be Responsible

Acknowledge that finding a responsible person to care for their baby when parents want or need to go out can be a challenge.
Brainstorm a list of characteristics parents want in a babysitter. The parenting information book has some ideas. Now think of how to find such a person—neighbors, friends, church, or other places.

Once the parents find a babysitter, both the babysitter and the baby (as much as he or she can understand) need to know what you expect, what the household rules are, and what to do in an emergency. Brainstorm ways to help provide the necessary information:

> How old is old enough to be a babysitter or for a child to be left alone? If this is an issue in the home, brainstorm with parents the characteristics a young person needs to babysit or stay home alone.

- Have the babysitter come early so you can take time to go over the rules and household.

- Write down all the important information and, after going over it with the sitter, post the information where it can be easily seen.

- Show the babysitter your home: where things are, how they work, etc. Encourage her to ask questions.

- Be sure the babysitter knows how to reach the parents and what to do in an emergency.

- What else…?

Do a role play with the home visitor in the role of a new babysitter.
Depending on the age of the child, involve him in the role play, too. Act out what the parents and babysitter should each ask and do before the parents leave. Begin by showing the home so the babysitter knows where things are. Continue by asking questions a sitter or parent might need to know.

Go over the handouts with parents and help them fill in the basic information.
Leave blank copies of the handouts so parents can use them again.

Activity 3: Childproofing Home, Car, and Baby's Area

Point out that the level of childproofing a home needs will depend on the age of the child, his temperament, other children in the home, and other factors.
Every child is different in her interest in exploring, in her abilities to open things, climb, etc. For some kids, a little barrier will discourage further exploration; for others, nailing the doors shut seems the only alternative that would work. Knowing each child is important.

Ages of siblings will affect childproofing, too. Older kids have different toys, needs, and activities than their younger siblings. It is important to balance the needs of older kids with the safety of all the children.

Brainstorm with the parents the level of childproofing they needed right now.
Then brainstorm the improvements in childproofing needed as their child grows. Home safety is important.

Do a child's-eye tour of the home to see what their child sees when he's at his level and what he could get into.
On your hands and knees, you and the parents go room-by-room, carefully examining the floor, the furniture, and the cupboards. Check the room's appliances, electric cords, electrical outlets, water sources—anything and everything. Encourage the parents to check even places and things that might seem unlikely. You and the parents may not like to dig in the trash, but to a toddler, it's a treasure chest of fun and forbidden.

Do a tour of every room.
The items below are listed by room, but parents can expect to find just about everything in every room at one time or another.

- **Living room** — outlets, breakable objects within reach, objects on the floor (little stones from shoes, pins, staples), tempting items not high enough, tablecloths to pull off tables, wastebaskets, coffee cups, game pieces, small toys, soda bottles, coins, alcohol left in glasses, cigarettes, matches, cigarette butts.

- **Kitchen** — outlets, stove, oven, pots on the stove, appliances, knives and forks and other pointy objects, cleaning supplies, dish soap, plants, refrigerator, sink, garbage can, plastic bags, string, batteries, rubber bands.

- **Bathroom** — hot water, toilet, trash can, medicine, vitamins, cosmetics, contact solutions, soap, shampoo, scissors, shoe polish, combs, hair dryers, curling irons, hot rollers, razors, bathtub, hair pins.

- **Bedroom** — outlets, coins, pins, buttons, lotions, plastic bags, cosmetics, bed (on top and under), hangers, jewelry, earrings.

If there is a garage and/or basement, include those in the tour. Look for chemicals, paints, gasoline, insecticides, cleaners, batteries, plants, poisons, tools, nails, tacks, machinery, etc.

Once you are done with the tour, talk about ways to make the home safer for their baby. Install any safety devices you have.

Go over the 20 safety rules in the parent book. Focus on the areas you notice the parents need help or that they have questions about.

Point out that it is important to keep their baby safe when away from home, too.
Visits to the grandparents or other homes can become hazardous. Before a visit, talk to the relative or friend about childproofing. A grandparent may have forgotten what a busy two-year-old can get into; a childless friend may not think of child safety the way you do.

Be sure to ask the older siblings for permission to look in their bags.

Remind the parents that another source of hazards is purses, tote bags, gym bags, and backpacks.
Many people carry medicines, cosmetics, coins, office supplies, hair pins, candy, and a lot of mysterious and enticing stuff in their handbags or other bags. Empty out your purse and briefcase or tote bag and the parents' and older siblings' backpacks or bags and look over what you find. Is there anything that is potentially hazardous? Remind parents to put visitors' bags up high and to keep parents' and siblings' bags out of reach, too.

Look at the car child safety seat (if appropriate).
If parents have a car, go out and look at the car seat and how it is installed. Is it installed correctly? If not, help the parents figure out how to install it so it works as it should. Follow all instructions when using a car seat. If necessary, call the car dealer to find out how to install the car seat correctly in their model of car. An incorrectly installed seat is dangerous and won't properly protect the child in an accident.

Many communities have car seat loan programs. If the family needs a car seat, help them find one through these resources. Remind parents that it's the law that every child under 40 pounds ride in a car seat. But law or not, it is the only safe way for a child to ride in the car.

Check for airbags, too.
Point out that an infant or child in a car seat should not be in the front. All children should always ride in the back seat when there are airbags on the passenger side of a car.

Remind the parents never to leave child alone in the car, in the car seat or out of it.
Cars are full of hazards and even young children can put a car in gear and cause it to roll into traffic. It also gets very hot in a car, even in cool weather. A baby can die in a car that's too hot or too cold.

You can demonstrate just how hot a car can get on a hot day by putting a candle or crayon in a disposable cup on the dashboard of a car and checking to see how long it takes to soften.
The melting point of most wax crayons and candles is about 130 degrees. A car can get this hot very quickly and a child can die of the heat. Even in cool weather, cars get hot.

Point out that toys can cause accidents, too.
Talk about what is a safe toy and what isn't. With parents, look at the toys in the house and rate each one for safety. Look for

- small parts that could cause choking

- toys that easily break and would have sharp edges

- toys with batteries

- electric toys

- painted toys that might have lead-based paint

- toys with long strings

- toys with rough or sharp edges or parts

- toys that are too old for the age of the child

Encourage the parents to discard any toys that are not safe.
Storing toys safely is important. Keep toys in an open box or basket without a cover. A cover could fall and hit baby or trap him in the box. Keep toys on a low shelf so the child won't be tempted to climb up to get them.

Parents may need help in finding ways to help their older kids play with Legos and other small toys while keeping younger children safe.

Discuss how parents can start to safety-proof their kids, too.
The age and development of a child affects how much she can understand about safety, but by the time she is between nine months and a year, parents can begin to teach ways to stay safe.

Ask the parents to put their baby on the floor so he can play.
Put something near the child that is safe, but pretend it is dangerous. For example, use a plastic cup, but pretend it is glass. With the parents,

watch their child carefully to see what he does. Does he grab for the glass, try to pick it up, put it in his mouth?

Now put down another safe "dangerous" object. Try a sheet of paper, but pretend it is a plastic bag. Ask parents to try to keep their child away from this new item. Encourage parents to try other things than saying, "No," or slapping hands. Talk about using distraction, moving the object, moving their child, and other ways.

Talk about ways to make a toddler or young child more safety-wise. Parents need to teach what's safe and what's not. It helps kids to understand why when parents teach respect for the body and explain some risks for the body. Parents need to model good safety themselves. But, how do parents teach these things?

Here are some ideas:

- Begin by using warning words—hot, ouch, sharp—and phrases—"Don't touch," "Be careful," "That could hurt you." You will need to repeat these over and over and over, but they will sink in and eventually your child will connect the words with dangerous situations.

- Act out things that might hurt. Touch a cup of hot coffee and then say, "HOT!" Do this often and with other things that are hot.

- Do the same with sharp objects, using a different warning word.

- Help a new walker learn about steps. Explain that they are off limits (and put up a gate), but let her climb up and down when the parents are there to help.

- Use warnings for electrical outlets (in addition to covering them up), and other hazards such as water.

- Any time he puts something other than food in his mouth, take it away and explain that it might hurt him. Establish rules about no running with something in his mouth—lollipop, pacifier.

- Talk about how to be careful when using a sharp knife or other potentially dangerous object.

Closing

Help parents summarize what they learned by going over these points. You may want to add others if you notice parents need more information.

- ✓ It is a good idea to post important phone numbers and information close to the phone for emergencies.
- ✓ There is a wide selection of safety equipment that can help prevent accidents if properly installed.
- ✓ Only leave your child in the care of responsible, safety-minded adults.
- ✓ Childproofing is very important. This means taking the time to look at their home as their child sees it, from her level, so any dangers can be fixed before accidents happen.

When Accidents Happen

What to Know First and Caring for an Injury

Getting Ready _____

Agenda

- **Opening:** be prepared for accidents
- **Keeping It Going:** how to care for an injured child
- **Closing:** using what we've learned

Objectives

Parents will

- be prepared in case of an accident
- learn first aid for simple injuries

In Advance

- Review the information in the parenting information book *Safe Child & Emergencies*.

Materials

Activity 2: Simple First Aid

- Young Family Parenting Information book *Safe Child & Emergencies* for parents
- First-aid supplies—band-aids, antiseptic, clean wash cloth, mild soap, etc. If possible, have some supplies you can leave with the parents.
- First-aid video and videoplayer. The video should include first aid for choking.

What to Know First and Caring for an Injury

Opening

"When an accident happens, parents can prevent more serious injuries by being calm and knowing what to do. Many injuries can be cared for at home, but parents need to know when injuries need professional attention, know when to call for help, and be ready to answer questions. Parents can learn first-aid techniques they can use before help arrives or for minor injuries. Having simple first-aid supplies on hand to treat minor cuts and scrapes and bumps makes it easier to calm and help their injured child."

Keeping It Going

Activity 1: Three Rules for an Emergency

Ask the parents to describe a childhood emergency they may have had.
It could have happened to them as a child, someone they saw, or to their own child.

- How did the adult in charge act?

- How did the child act?

- How do the parents think they would respond to an accident involving their child?

Remind the parents not to wait for an accident to happen to find out what to do.

Go over the three rules for an emergency in the parenting information book.
Ask the parents if they have talked to their health care provider about when to call the office and when to go to the hospital emergency room. If they haven't, suggest they do so before an accident happens and they are in a panic.

Rehearse what steps they should take in an emergency.
Who should they call, what should they say on the phone, how would they comfort their child, etc.

In spite of caution and preparation, all kids have accidents at one time or another. Knowing when to call the health care provider, going to the emergency room, or calling 911 are important so an injured child gets the care they need, when they need it.

Point out that some situations are obviously emergencies.
Some examples of an emergency are

- child is having a problem breathing or is turning blue or choking
- bleeding cannot be controlled
- a bone is sticking out through the skin
- child is unconscious or unresponsive
- child has swallowed poison or other non-food substance

Talk about whom and when to call in an accident or emergency.
Call 911 or the local emergency number. In case of poisoning, call the Poison Control Center. They will tell you what to do.

Role play making an emergency call to 911 or the Poison Control Center.
In an emergency, parents can be flustered or confused. If possible, arrange for someone at your office to play the role of dispatcher, so the parents can talk to a real person they can't see. Call the number for them, but let them talk once the "dispatcher" is on. Decide before you call what the emergency is. Have the dispatcher ask questions like these:

- What is your name and address?
- What's wrong?
- What is the baby's age?
- The Poison Control Center will ask what the baby ate. Have the container or whatever it was, like a plant at hand, during the call.

Follow the instructions of the dispatcher.

Tell the parents that some injuries may not be so obvious, such as a bump on the head, or obviously serious.

The Young Family Parenting Information book *Healthy Child/Sick Child* has information on calling the health care provider, too.

When in doubt, call the health care provider and ask what to do. They want to help parents do the right thing. You can talk about the following situations or ask the parents what they want to know.

- A child should be watched after a heavy bump on the head or blow to the stomach. Any changes in behavior, severe bruising, vomiting, unusual sleepiness, failure to respond, or other changes in appearance are reasons to get medical attention.

- Some kids are allergic to common insect bites and everyone needs emergency help if bitten by a poisonous spider or snake (black widow, brown recluse, scorpion, etc.). Difficulty breathing is a sign that emergency help is needed. If the parents live in an area where there are poisonous insects or reptiles, they need to be able to identify these creatures. They also need to learn ways to avoid them inside and outside.

- It may not be possible to tell if a bone is broken. It's a myth that it's not broken if you can move it. Persistent pain (continued crying is a clue), numbness/tingling (feeling "funny"), swelling, deformity, or inability to bear weight on the injured part are signs of broken bones. Call the health care provider. Compound fractures (bone is sticking through skin) are always an emergency. Call the health care provider or go to the hosptial emergency room.

- When to get stitches is often a question. Large or jagged cuts that bleed profusely or won't stop bleeding should be looked at by a health care professional. Call for instructions about whether to go to the health care provider or or hosptial emergency room.

- All animal and human bites should be looked at by a health professional.

Continue discussing the types of injuries that call for emergency help, a call to the doctor, or a visit to the emergency room until parents feel comfortable they can handle an emergency.

Activity 2: Simple First Aid

Remind parents that they can treat some minor injuries at home if they have the experience and proper supplies.
Assemble supplies for a simple first aid kit. Look for band-aids, a clean wash cloth, soap, antiseptic (like Bactine), cotton balls, tweezers, rubbing alcohol to sterilize tweezers, gauze pads, adhesive tape, and an ice pack.

Help parents find a container in the house to put the supplies in, such as a toolbox, old lunch box, big cookie tin, fanny pack, or zipper plastic bag.
The container needs to be big enough to hold the supplies yet small enough to carry to the site of an accident. Scrub the container and dry it well. Arrange the supplies in the container so they are easy to reach. Keep the supplies together and stored out of children's reach.

Look for alternatives to standard supplies and equipment, too.
No ice pack? Keep a wet sponge or wash cloth frozen in the freezer or use an unopened package of frozen peas. Ice in a cloth or plastic bag will work, too. No gauze? Use a feminine napkin or clean diaper to put pressure on bleeding. Ask the parents to suggest other alternatives to standard supplies.

Watch a video on first-aid techniques, including choking and simple wound care.
Discuss what you have seen with the parents. Continue the discussion by asking the parents questions like these:

- Do you think you could handle an emergency involving your child? Another child?

- What first-aid techniques are new to you?

Go over the first-aid techniques in the parenting information book and those in the video.
If the parents agree and the baby seems cooperative, have parents practice the first-aid techniques on their baby. Most older children will enjoy being bandaged up in play. Demonstrate how to clean a cut or scrape, what to do for a minor burn, how to wash out the eyes, and how to remove a splinter. Encourage the parents to try these techniques, too. The baby may be happy to play along if she gets to wear a lot of band-aids, but probably won't enjoy having water poured in her eyes. Use your judgment when involving the baby.

Reaffirm the parents' ability to prevent accidents and injuries and to care for a child who does have an accident. One of the best ways to care for an injured child is for the parents to keep calm and to soothe the child.

Remind the parents that first aid is help given at the time of the injury before professional help arrives.
In case of a true emergency (see Three Rules for an Emergency), check the condition of the injured person and call for help. Dial 911 or ask someone else to call and then perform first aid until help arrives.

Reassure the parents that they will be able to handle most childhood injuries and accidents at home.
For most, first aid from the parents is enough. Because the parents know what to do in an emergency and are prepared to do it, their children will be safer.

Closing

Help parents summarize what they learned by going over these points. You may want to add others if you notice parents need more information.

- ✓ It helps everyone if the parents remain calm during an emergency.
- ✓ Know when to get medical help and when a minor injury can be treated at home.
- ✓ Be prepared and calm when calling for help or information.
- ✓ Help the child keep calm by holding her and speaking in a soft, soothing voice.
- ✓ Parents can learn simple first-aid techniques that can be used in case of an accident or injury.
- ✓ Keeping first-aid supplies like band-aids and antiseptic on hand and easy to find makes helping an injured child easier and faster.

Handout

Ready to Go:
Preparing the Sitter and the Children

Everyone benefits when time is taken to help prepare the babysitter and children for times when parents are not at home. Here are things to talk about and write down before you leave.

For the sitter...

General information
- your whole name, address, and phone number of the location the sitter is at—she may not know this or forget it in an emergency
- where you will be (name, address, and phone number) and when you will return
- emergency numbers and who to call for help
- what to do regarding safety, emergencies, etc.
- the location of the nearest pay phone, if necessary
- information about any medication that needs to be given and location of first-aid supplies

House information
- how to operate appliances, fire extinguisher, etc.
- where light switches are located
- how to lock doors and where to find keys
- peculiarities—tricky toilets, funny noises, etc.

Food
- your expectations about cooking, meals, and snacks—what, when, and where

Clothing
- where clean clothes and pajamas can be found
- how your baby should be diapered, where the supplies are and how to clean up when the sitter is done

Comforting, guidance, and discipline
- ways your baby likes to be helped, ideas to try that have worked best for you and others
- your baby's typical behavior and a bit about the developmental stage of your child
- behavior that requires discipline as well as behavior not to worry about
- discipline methods to use and not to use—explain some details of how you do the comforting, guiding, or disciplining.

Routines
- bathtime, bedtime, mealtime, naps, etc.

Special toys, games, snacks

Other expectations and rules
- for the child—snacks, activities, behavior, bedtime
- for the sitter—phone, TV, homework, food, visitors, cleaning up

(continued)

And for your child...

- Have the sitter meet your child a day or so before you need to be gone.

- Have the sitter come a little early so you have time to explain things and so your baby gets to see that you are comfortable with and trust the sitter. Rushing out the door right away is scary for kids when they aren't used to a new babysitter.

- Consider a special plaything or activity for the sitter to do with your child.

- Help your child and babysitter warm up to each other before you go.

- Let your child know that you are leaving— sneaking out is not fair. But, be careful not to overdo the good-byes. Be brief, upbeat, and loving.

Babysitter's Checklist

Child(ren) Name/age: _____

Name/age: _____

Parent's name: _____

Home address: _____

Phone number (of home or closest neighbor): _____

Nearest pay phone, if necessary: _____

Place parent will be: _____

_____ Phone number: _____

Time of return: _____

Emergency: Call 911 first. (There is no charge for 911 calls made from a pay phone.) Then, if possible, call the parents.

Someone parent trusts to help babysitter with a problem:

Name _____ Phone number: _____

This person is a: ❏ family member ❏ friend ❏ neighbor ❏ _____

Health care provider: _____

Phone number: _____ Medical record number: _____

Medicine: Who _____ What _____

When _____ How much _____

Other _____

Meals: When _____ What _____

_____

Snacks: When _____ What _____

_____

Naptime: When _____ Where _____

Routine _____

Bath: Routine _____

Bedtime: When _____ Where _____

Routine _____

Other: _____

_____

_____

Chapter 5
Baby Grows

Getting to Know Your Baby

Helping Baby

Introduction

Home Visitor Information

This is one of the most important books in this series (the other is *Baby Plays*). Parents have many sources of information on taking care of their baby's physical needs, including the other books of this series, but with *Baby Grows*, you have an opportunity to show parents the importance of understanding child development and to help them find ways to encourage their baby to develop into a healthy, happy, strong child.

You can help parents understand that all babies are different and that each one has a unique personality and temperament, just as adults do. Even more, you can help the parents understand their own baby's personality and temperament and how, by understanding their baby, they will be able to find ways to meet his physical and emotional needs.

You have a wonderful opportunity to model the behavior and activities that help parents help their baby. Whenever you are interacting with their baby, remember that the parents are watching and learning. You can describe what you are doing, point out how the baby is reacting, suggest other ways to do things, and give many other ideas parents may need to understand what they can do.

In the long run, it won't matter much if parents use cloth or disposable diapers or use liquid soap or bar soap. Yes, it is important that parents take excellent care of all their baby's physical needs, but what really matters in the end is how they do this. It is the daily, loving interaction with their baby that shows how much parents love him and how much they want him to grow up into a healthy, happy person. It shows in how parents change diapers, feed their baby, play with her, put her to bed, soothe her cries. When parents respond to their baby's needs immediately, talk and coo at him, take time to get to know what he likes and dislikes, and take those likes and dislikes into consideration in all their dealings with their baby, that is when parents know they are doing all they can to help their baby grow.

After the activities in *Baby Grows*, parents will

- understand how babies are different from adults

- know the importance of daily routines for babies

- know how to observe their baby to help him develop

- know how babies change and grow

- know some ways to encourage their baby's development

- understand that the very first step in learning about guiding and disciplining a child is to learn about child development

- know the importance of consistent, loving discipline to help their child learn and grow

- understand that discipline is guiding and teaching a child about the best ways to behave

- know the signs of when a child is physically and emotionally ready to be toilet trained

- begin to establish a sleep routine to help their child understand what to expect at bedtime, and feel safe and relaxed so the parents and child can enjoy bedtime

Important Information for Home Visitors

- A baby is not the same as her parents or other adults in the family. When parents know how babies are different from adults or older children, they can help their baby grow best.

- A baby grows best when her parents do the same things each day (a *daily routine*). A baby feels safe and loved when the family has routines. A baby may feel upset or worried when too many things change.

- No two babies are exactly the same—even babies who are the same age or from the same family. It's okay for one baby to be different from another baby. Each baby is a special and unique person.

- As babies grow, they change in many ways, including eating, sleeping, diapering, expression of feelings, playing, communicating, and, of course, size.

- Discipline is about guiding and teaching the preferred way for a child to behave. Discipline may include changing behaviors parents do not like. Discipline helps a child to learn and to grow.

- Discipline is **not** spanking, hitting, hurting, yelling, or shutting a child in a room alone.

- The best way for parents to guide and discipline their children is to learn about child development so their expectations are appropriate. Other ways are to childproof; distract; say "no;" use clear, simple rules; be a good role model; be consistent; and teach, recognize, and praise good behavior.

- Young babies (birth to six months old) **cannot** intentionally misbehave, but young babies may do things that parents don't want them to do. Older babies (seven to 24 months old) may misbehave for many different reasons.

- Time-out is one way to discipline a child who is at least 18 months of age or older. Time-out is putting the child in a special (but safe) place where someone can still see the child. The child is to sit quietly and wait until a brief time-out is over (usually one minute for each year of age).

- Toilet training should not begin until age two to 2-1/2 years. A child has to be physically and emotionally ready before he can be toilet trained.

- Parents and their child decide when it's time to start toilet training. Parents can know when their child is ready by watching for the signs that indicate readiness. Begin toilet training when the child is ready, the parents and child are not sick or tired, the parents aren't too busy, and when the child is being cooperative in other areas and is interested in learning.

- The best way to help children get to sleep is to have a "sleep routine," which is quite simply doing the same things at the same time whenever baby goes to bed. Sleep routines help children know what to expect at bedtime, feel safe and relaxed, and enjoy bedtime.

- Sleep routines are especially important for older babies (12 to 24 months).

- When a baby has trouble going to sleep or wakes up during the night, parents need to find out why their baby can't sleep and then give their baby the help she needs to get to sleep.

Additional Topic Information

Your Baby Is a Person

Each person is an unique individual. Think about someone who is close to you. Are you able to do exactly the same things? Do you both like the same foods? Do you both wear the same kind of clothes? Do you like to do the same things for relaxation? Chances are you don't do things exactly the same as this person.

The same holds true for babies. Each baby is unique. Each baby has his own temperament or personality. Babies have different needs, likes, dislikes, and ways of operating in the world than parents have. Babies think and learn differently than parents. Parents need to remember that babies aren't just small adults.

It's important for parents to learn that babies are different from each other, even from babies of the same age or in the same family. This doesn't mean that one baby is better than another. It doesn't mean that a baby who can't do certain things is "bad," nor is a baby "bad" whose temperament is different from what the parents would like it to be. Parents need to accept that every person is unique and that their baby is a special person in her own right.

You can help parents accept their child for who he is. If parents are worried about their baby's temperament or other characteristics, you can try to find out why. You can help parents view their baby in a positive way. You can help them use positive words to describe their baby by using these words yourself. For example, if parents are describing their baby as "hard to handle," you can talk about the baby as being very active or curious. Talk about how those behaviors will help the baby later in life. For example, a curious baby could grow up to be a scientist. An active baby could grow up to become an athlete. This is another place to talk about child development, too. Some behaviors may be related to a developmental stage. For example, a baby who is just learning to walk will want to walk all the time. He may struggle and fuss to get down from the grocery cart because he wants to walk, not ride. He has realized there is a new view of the world now that he can walk, and he wants to be part of it! This doesn't mean he has a "different" temperament; it means he is at a new stage of development and his parents must adjust to it.

Parents can learn a lot about their baby from watching her. Parents can think about how their baby acts at certain times. These can be clues to help parents understand their baby better and to learn to accept their baby as a person.

Parents can tolerate many more changes in their daily lives than babies can. Parents may be able to eat at a different time each day or go to sleep at very different times each day, but a baby needs these things to stay pretty much the same each day. Babies need routines.

Babies grow best when there are routines in the family. A routine can be doing the same thing at the same time each day, for example, putting the baby to bed at 8:00 p.m. each night. A routine also can be doing the same thing each time you do a certain activity, for example, every time the baby goes to bed a parent can rock and sing to the baby.

When there are routines in a baby's life, she will be able to know what to expect each day. Routines help babies grow well, to learn to trust the world, and to learn how the world works. Without a routine, everything can seem to be a surprise for a baby. Babies like consistency. They don't like to have everything be new and different everyday. He may become agitated all the time. Even if a family is experiencing a lot of change or stress, parents and others in the family should try to keep as many routines as possible the same for the baby.

Baby Changes

Human growth and development is an amazing and very complicated process. A baby's physical, mental, emotional, and social development all happen at the same time. Babies grow and change very quickly. Babies learn new things almost daily. Watching a baby grow and develop is an exciting part of being new parents.

Each baby follows the same general pattern of development. For example, babies usually will first learn how to hold up their heads, then roll over, sit up, crawl, walk with help, and then walk without help. However, each baby grows at his own pace. One baby may sit up at seven months while another baby may not sit up until he is almost nine months old. This is normal. Remind parents that when they see lists or charts of when babies "should" do things, these are approximate ages. There is a wide range of normal.

Sometimes when a baby is working very hard on one area of development, he may not be working very hard on another area. When a baby is learning to walk, for example, he may not make much progress in learning to talk. This is normal.

Parents need to understand how babies develop. It's important that parents not expect too much too soon or too little too late in terms of their baby's development. By expecting too much, parents will have unrealistic expectations about what their baby can or cannot do. Parents may push their baby to do things she can't do, or they may think their baby is just stubborn and won't do what they want. This can make parents angry or unhappy with their baby and affect the parent-child relationship. It's important that parents understand all areas of child development so they know when a child can realistically be expected to control an impulse to touch, for example. This helps parents understand their child's behavior and will affect how they may discipline the child or teach her other things.

If parents expect too little, they may miss a sign that something isn't normal development. If a baby is very slow—months behind what the charts say, for example—to walk or talk or crawl or climb, then parents need to check with their health care professional to see if their baby is okay.

Parents need to know what changes to expect and when they are likely to happen. When parents have a basic understanding of child development, they will be able to better understand their child, know that their child is developing normally, enhance their child's development, and know when to talk to someone if they have concerns.

If parents have concerns about their baby's development, you can help them deal with these concerns. You can help them identify developmental milestones that will show them their baby is developing normally. You also can help them know whether they need to talk to their health care provider about their concerns.

Encourage parents to keep a record of their baby's development. One way parents can do this is to get some kind of a baby book. There are many different ones published commercially, or parents can make one. Meld offers *Beginnings: Your Baby's Story* a book which can help track a baby's developmental milestones

In the baby book, parents can record when their child reaches certain milestones of development. This helps parents see how their baby is developing. Plus, their baby will enjoy looking at it with her parents when she is older.

As you plan your visit, keep in mind that the information in *Baby Grows* isn't intended to be a detailed chart of growth and development. The purpose is to give parents an idea of what changes to expect and when. Many books are available that offer more detailed information about growth and development.

Along with talking about what changes to expect, you can give parents ideas for enhancing their baby's development. You can use some of the ideas in the handouts during the visit or for "homework" for the parents. Remind parents that the little things mean a lot. It's not playing with toys that will help their baby develop, it's playing and interacting with parents, siblings, grandparents, and others. Parents (and others) can encourage the baby to stretch her muscles and her brain by playing games, singing and talking, taking her places that have things to see, touch, smell, or hear. Remember to tell parents it's never too early to read to their baby. Babies enjoy the closeness of sitting with a parent, hearing the parent's voice, seeing the pictures, and touching the book. Reading opens a baby's world.

Over the course of your visits, you may want to come back often to the topic of growth and development. You might have a periodic "check in" to give parents the opportunity to talk about questions and concerns and to help parents keep in mind the milestones their baby will be reaching soon.

As you talk about growth and development, there are several things you can do to help parents. You can allow the parents to take pride in their child's development. You can help parents accept their child's own pace of development. You can help parents see their child as special and unique.

Discipline

Discipline may be a topic of interest to parents as their baby grows. During your visits, you can begin to help parents think about discipline and how they will deal with their child's behavior. You can guide them through the process of looking back at how they were disciplined as children, which may be painful to do, to help them determine how they want to discipline their child. Help parents consider a wide variety of discipline methods and choose those appropriate for their own family.

Discipline can be a very difficult issue for parents to think or talk about. Some parents may have been very severely disciplined as children. They may not know that there are alternatives to hitting or yelling because that is the only kind of "discipline" they have ever known or seen. Parents may not be aware of child abuse laws in the United States that prohibit some forms of physical punishment. Other parents may never been disciplined at all. Whatever the case, help parents understand that their role as parents is to help their child live in the world. One way they do this is through discipline. The challenge parents face is to look at their own upbringing and culture and decide which values, ideas, and behaviors they will continue with their own family and which they will choose not to continue. (As a home visitor, this may be a good time to review the laws in your state regarding mandated reporting of possible child maltreatment.)

Parents may need to examine their expectations for their child's behavior and learn how to decide if these expectations are too high. Understanding child development helps parents have realistic expectations about their child's behavior. This understanding of how a child can be expected to behave can make it easier for parents to prevent or deal with unwanted behaviors. Parents need to understand that there is a difference between "misbehavior" and unwanted behavior. *Misbehavior* can only occur when a child is at the stage of mental development that enables her to choose a way to behave. Parents may not want their child to grab candy at the grocery store, but until he can control the impulse to grab (around three years of age or later), it's not misbehavior to grab the candy.

There are many methods and styles of discipline. When a child is very young, the way parents *discipline*—or change unwanted behavior—is usually to change the situation. Parents can distract their baby from the unwanted behavior by offering her a toy or playing with her. They can physically move their baby away from the situation. They can change the environment (childproofing) so their baby doesn't get into unwanted situations.

As their baby grows and develops, there will be many other ways parents can discipline. Starting when baby is around 18 months of age or so, parents can try time-outs. Parents will set limits, praise their child's good behavior, teach the behavior they want, and more. Parents will learn which methods work best with their child.

Having many options to consider can be both positive and negative for parents. It's positive because parents can choose discipline methods that are appropriate for their child's development and enhance development and self-esteem. However, parents are faced with many other decisions.

Parents must take into account many factors in choosing a particular discipline method to use at a given time.

For some parents, spanking may be their first reaction to any situation calling for discipline. In general, spanking or hitting a child is not an effective discipline method. Spanking may get immediate results, but it doesn't teach a child why he should change his behavior or how to change it. Children need help from their parents to understand why a behavior is unacceptable and help in changing the behavior. Spanking is especially ineffective with babies and very young children. It confuses them when someone they love hurts them. They don't yet understand misbehavior, so spanking is a real mystery to them. Help parents find more suitable and successful discipline methods.

Before parents can understand why their child misbehaves, they need to understand a few things about all children.

Children naturally want to please their parents. Children understand at a very early age that they need their parents to give them love, comfort, warmth, food, and pleasure. Children depend on their parents. Children want to be with their parents more than any other human beings in the world.

In children's eyes, parents are very powerful. Parents are bigger, wiser, older, stronger. Parents know how to make a child feel safe, secure, and happy. Children sense that their parents are very powerful. Parents don't need to spank or yell to demonstrate their power.

Children misbehave for a lot of different reasons. Babies don't know right from wrong. They are curious and want to explore and try new things. Young children don't know what things are safe or good for them and what things may not be safe. They must be taught these things. Young children can't think about the consequences of their behavior before they do something and they often forget things that have happened to them in the past.

Children have very strong impulses. Children can't control their impulses until age three or older. Young children do not have patience. They respond immediately to things that are happening or to what they feel. Parents need to guide their children through problem situations so that they will learn self-control.

Children need love and respect, just like adults. Children are people, too, with feelings, self-esteem, and a sense of pride. Parents need to learn to discipline in such a way that their children can maintain their dignity and value as people.

Children need to feel worthwhile and loved. Children need to know that no matter what they do, their parents still love, value, and accept them. Discipline must be carried out in the context of a loving relationship between parent and child.

Parents also need to feel worthwhile and loved. Learning to discipline a child is a very difficult task. As a home visitor, you can support and encourage the parents when they feel confused, frustrated, and lost.

Help parents keep in mind that the goal of discipline is to help children learn how to control their own behavior without damaging their self-esteem.

Here are some suggestions that may help parents in disciplining their child:

- **Parents need to be very specific** with their child. They need to tell her exactly what they don't want her to do and exactly what they do want her to do. For example, telling a child to be a "good girl" doesn't tell the child what she can or can't do.

- **Parents need to follow through** on what they've told their child. If parents tell their child that he will get a time-out if he continues to hit another child and, if he does hit again, the parents need to give him a time-out.

- **Parents need to be consistent.** If parents don't want their child to play with the television, then each time the child does so, the parent must discipline the child. Parents and other family members should try to be consistent with each other. They should try to agree on how a child will be disciplined for a certain behavior so that the child will be disciplined the same way by each person.

Sometimes children do things that make parents very angry. Parents who are tired or experiencing a lot of stress may reach breaking points when their child misbehaves. Parents need to remember that there will be times when they will feel like they are at the end of their ropes in dealing with their child. **Before they get to their breaking point**, parents need to think about ways to handle their anger without hurting themselves or their child.

If parents reach the point where they may hurt their baby out of anger, there are things they can do. Parents can

- put the baby in a safe place (like a crib or playpen) and go to another place in the house

- call or visit a friend, relative, or neighbor to talk about what they're feeling

- ask a friend, relative, or trusted neighbor to watch the baby for awhile so they can have a break

- bring the baby to a "crisis nursery," where someone will watch the baby so the parent can get away for awhile

Your visits can serve as a source of information about why young babies do things that parents don't like and why children misbehave as they get older. The visit can provide a safe place for parents to discuss their questions, concerns, behavior, and any conflicts they're having with family members who disagree with their methods of discipline. This combination of information and support will enable parents to understand their child's behavior, learn about methods to deal with misbehavior, develop their own styles of discipline, and know that they're not alone in dealing with these difficult issues.

Toilet Training

Children's minds and bodies need to be ready before they can be successfully toilet trained. Children need to be able to control their bowel and bladder movements in order to use a toilet. They need to be aware of when they have to go to the bathroom. Parents who know the signs that indicate readiness for toilet training and wait to begin until the signs are there will have an easier, more successful experience than those who don't follow the signs.

Many parents feel pressured, either by themselves or by others, to start toilet training their child at an early age. Some may want to get their child out of diapers to save money or to end diaper changing. Some may feel that, in order to be "good" or "successful" parents, their child should be trained very early. Decisions about toilet training, like so many other parenting decisions, must involve what is best for that family. Many well-meaning relatives and friends may suggest the "perfect time" for parents to start toilet training. Parents need to learn to trust their own knowledge of their child. They know their child best and they will be the best judge of when their child is ready to begin toilet training. Parents should only begin when their child seems ready and they can spend the time that is necessary to successfully toilet train.

Starting toilet training too early can lead to frustration and anger for both parents and child. Encourage parents to watch their child for signs of readiness.

Parents need to recognize the fact that, even though a child may be physically ready, she will have "accidents." Children can get very involved in games or activities and realize too late that they need to go to the bathroom. Children may have trouble waking up at night or be afraid to go to the bathroom in the dark, which may result in them wetting their beds. One thing parents can do during this time of learning is to be patient and understanding with their child, especially if she wets her pants or bed.

The purpose of this section is to help parents learn the signs that show their child is ready to start toilet training. As a home visitor, you can help ease the parents' concerns about dealing with family members or friends who may be pressuring them to start toilet training before their child is ready. You can encourage them to seek out sources of information and support when their child is ready for toilet training.

Naptime/Bedtime

One of the most important things that will help a child stay healthy and grow well is sleep. One way parents can make sure their baby enjoys going to sleep and has few problems in getting to sleep is by having a sleep routine.

Babies like to know what is going to happen and they like to have things stay the same. A sleep routine is a sign to a baby that it's time to go to sleep. It helps a baby to relax and feel safe because the sleep routine is the same night after night. Developing a sleep routine is a way for parents and their baby to share love and feel very close to each other as they close another day together.

For adults, it can be hard to go to sleep right after an exciting event, like a party, game, or special celebration. Most adults take time to unwind and relax before they go to sleep. Just like adults, babies need to get ready to go to sleep. As a home visitor, you can help parents be aware that they need to help their baby get ready to go to sleep. Taking time to help their baby go to sleep will help the baby get to sleep without any problems and to stay asleep during the night.

Families may experience a lot of change and stress. Parents may worry about jobs or money. Families may have to move frequently or live with many other people. These stresses and changes can make it hard for their baby to sleep well. However, even when there is stress or when things change a lot, parents can still keep their baby's sleep routine as much the same as possible.

When a baby has trouble getting to sleep, parents may become frustrated. They may want their child in bed at a certain time so they can have some peace and quiet for themselves. They may feel like they're not good parents if they can't get their baby to sleep. If sleep problems continue, bedtime can become an angry time for both parents and child.

This section will show parents that they can do a lot of simple, soothing, relaxing things with their baby to help her calm down and get ready for bed. Parents need to learn what to look for if their baby has trouble getting to sleep or if she wakes up during the night. Parents need to remember that just as adults have trouble sleeping sometimes, babies do, too. Parents need to be patient to help their baby through these difficult nights.

Sleep routines need to change as a baby gets older. For instance, a young baby might enjoy being rocked to sleep. An older child might enjoy looking at a book or putting a puzzle together before bed. As their child grows, parents can try new things to make sleep routines fun and relaxing.

The goal is to keep bedtime a happy, pleasant, soothing time. Parents can prevent the majority of sleep problems by repeating sleep routines every day, being firm about their baby staying in bed, and being aware of what might be keeping their baby awake.

Concerns to Be Aware of During Home Visits

If you do notice any of these concerns, discuss them with the parents and/or your supervisor. Your supervisor will help you decide what needs to be done.

- Parents who expect their baby to act like an adult.
- Parents who are having trouble keeping any kind of a routine for their baby's daily life.
- Parents who compare their baby with other babies and think that their baby is bad because he is different.
- Parents who don't accept their baby's temperament.
- Parents who think their baby should be doing things he isn't old enough to do.
- A baby that is slow in her development, and parents who don't see it or don't know what to do about it.
- Parents who think their baby is misbehaving, even though the baby is less than seven months old.
- Parents who use only yelling or spanking as discipline methods with their young child.
- Parents who are using very severe physical punishment.
- Parents who don't do anything when their child misbehaves because they don't care or because they don't know what to do.
- Parents who are starting toilet-training too early.
- Parents who are emotionally upset and very frustrated with the toilet-training process.

- Parents who punish toilet-training "accidents."
- A child who seems to be resisting all toilet-training efforts.
- A child who doesn't seem to be able to relax and calm down before going to sleep.
- Parents who seem tired all the time because their child is up during the night.
- Parents who get very angry when their child will not go to sleep.

Getting to Know Your Baby

Your Baby Is a Person

Getting Ready _____

Agenda

- **Opening:** getting to know your baby
- **Keeping It Going:** your baby's temperament
- **Closing:** using what we've learned

Objectives

Parents will

- understand how babies are different from adults
- discuss the importance of daily routines for babies
- learn to observe their baby to see all the things they can learn

In Advance

- Review the information in the parenting information book *Baby Grows*.

Materials

Activity 1: Babies and Parents are Different

- Young Family Parenting Information book *Baby Grows* for parents
- pictures of babies at different ages and various adults
- pictures representing different parts of daily life, including eating and food, growth, learning, feelings, play, and other activities people do regularly (magazines are good sources for both sets of pictures)

Activity 2: Routines

- paper and pencil

Getting Ready (continued)

Activity 3: Know Your Baby

- copies of the Baby's Temperament checklist from the *Baby Grows* parent book

Your Baby Is a Person

Opening

"Babies are different from parents. Parents can do far more than babies can. Each baby is unique, different from all other babies. Getting to know what their baby can do and figuring out her temperament can help parents understand their baby's behavior and reactions."

Keeping It Going

Activity 1: Babies and Parents Are Different

Bring the baby into the visit with you and the parents.
Put the baby on the floor in a safe place. Give the baby some toys or something else to play with.

Encourage the parents to observe what their child is doing.
Help them talk about what they see by asking a few questions like these. Use the baby's name whenever possible in the questions.

- Does (the baby) immediately reach for the toy? Does (the baby) seem more cautious approaching the toy?

- What does (the baby) do first with the toy?

- Does the toy seem to hold (the baby's) interest?

- Do you think (the baby) would act the same or different if the toy were one he had never seen before?

- What else do you see (the baby) doing?

Continue talking about what the baby is doing and what the parents learn from watching their baby.
Remind parents how much they have learned from watching their baby grow since birth.

Go over the information in *Baby Grows* parent book.
Talk about ways a baby is different from his parents. Use the pictures as a way to get the discussion going.

You can ask parents if they have noticed how different a sibling's development has been from this baby's. Remember, this isn't a contest; it's a way to remind parents how much they learn from observing their children.

Use the pictures of food, for example, to talk about what babies can and should eat compared to what parents can eat.
Continue using the pictures to talk about how parents are different from their baby. Babies are growing and changing far more than adults are. Babies learn things in different ways, express their feelings differently than adults, etc.

Use different pictures of babies to talk about how babies are not all the same.
Continue by asking about parents and other adults. Use the pictures of the adults. Ask questions like these:

- Do all adults look the same?
- Do adults all like the same foods?
- Do adults like the same kinds of entertainment?

Remind parents that not all adults are the same either. Each person is a unique individual and different personality traits show up even in babies.

Activity 2: Routines

Ask the parents whether or not they prefer to have routines in their lives or if they prefer less structure in schedules for waking up, eating, or other daily activities.
Continue by asking how they feel if their daily routine changes.

You may want to remind parents that even if they find a routine "boring" and they like a lot of changes in their day, babies benefit from having a routine. Routines make babies feel secure.

Tell the parents that even though each baby is different, every baby will benefit from having regular routines.
Routines help a baby adjust to changes in his growth or environment because he understands that certain things happen when other things happen. For example, after eating in the morning, he knows a bath is coming when he hears water running. Knowing what will happen next makes a baby feel more comfortable and secure. Most babies like life to be predictable.

Family routines need to work for all family members. Ask how the siblings' routines might affect the baby's routine. Is the new baby more adaptable to change than their other babies were? Why might this be?

Ask the parents to describe a typical day at home with their baby. Write down their description.
You may want to have them walk through what happens at what time of day.

- Do things usually happen at the same time each day—meals, baths, naps, and other daily activities?
- Have the parents noticed anything different about their baby if routines change?

Too much change in a baby's day can make him upset and worried. He may not eat or sleep if there is too much change.

Point out that routines make a baby feel secure. Brainstorm with the parents some reasons for having things happen in a regular pattern to help their baby feel secure.
Here are some ideas:

- A baby knows that her parents care for her when they take care of her needs regularly.

- Most babies don't like surprises. They like the feel of a steady routine—eat first, bath next, or whatever the schedule.

- Babies feel secure when they know what will happen next.

Ask the parents if they want help in establishing a routine for their baby.
Discuss their typical day and help the parents map out some ways to start a routine. Encourage them to begin with small changes first and keep going until they have a routine that works for them and their baby. Make a schedule with the parents so they can follow what they want to do.

If there are many changes to make or changes parents can't control, concentrate on what a parent can turn into a routine.
Even if their baby must sleep in a different place every night, the routine leading up to bedtime can be the same each evening. Help the parents figure out a bedtime routine that can be done anywhere.

Activity 3: Know Your Baby

Sit with the parents and admire their baby.
Comment on how different she is from other babies—how special and delightful. Remind parents that no two babies are the same. Each one is unique.

Remind parents that figuring out what their baby likes and doesn't like, how she reacts to things, what makes her cry, and other things about her can make it easier for parents to help.
How a baby acts or how she is as a person is called temperament. Each baby reacts differently to different things. Every person, adult or child, has a temperament. Our temperament often shows in how we first react to something.

> You will have a sense of how much of a routine is possible in the home. If there is a lot of change all the time, work with the parents to try to establish calming routines wherever possible. Bedtime often is a good place to start a routine.

Help parents understand that it is important to be aware of their own temperaments and that of their baby, as well as how the temperaments work together.
Siblings' and parents' temperaments may match or be different from one another. Getting along with people of different temperaments can take some work and adjustments.

A quiet temperament baby with an active temperament parent may have trouble adjusting. Parents may need to change how they interact with their baby by being calmer and not as active. It is up to the parents to recognize what needs to be done and make the changes because their baby cannot.

Use the questions and checklist in the Baby's Temperament checklist to help parents think about their baby's temperament.
Bring the baby into the visit so parents can observe or try out some of the activities to see how their baby reacts.

Closing

Help parents summarize what they learned by going over these points. You may want to add others if you notice parents need more information.

✓ Routines help babies by giving them a feeling of security that things will be the same. A lot of change can upset a baby.

✓ Babies are not "little adults." They are different from parents in what they need and what they can do.

✓ Every baby is different from every other baby, even twins or siblings, and different from adults, too.

✓ Parents who watch their babies and learn as much as they can about them will be able to help their babies grow best.

✓ Every person, including babies, has a temperament that is unique to that person. Parents can determine their baby's temperament, which will help them understand their baby better.

Baby Changes

Getting Ready

Agenda

- **Opening:** all babies are different
- **Keeping It Going:** how babies grow and change
- **Closing:** using what we've learned

Objectives

Parents will

- learn how babies change and grow
- know some ways to encourage their baby's development

In Advance

- Review the information in the parenting information book *Baby Grows*.

Materials

Activity 1: Changes

- Young Family Parenting Information book *Baby Grows* for parents
- copies of the charts in the "Babies Change" topic in the parent book
- paper
- crayons or markers
- locate a nearby park, playground, or recreation center to visit for this activity

Activity 2: Encouraging Physical Development

- beach ball
- copy of Helping Baby Grow Strong handout at the end of this section

Baby Changes

Opening

"Babies grow and change all the time. If we watch our babies, we can tell a lot about their development. Parents can encourage learning and physical development through play and interaction with their baby."

Keeping It Going

Activity 1: Changes

Go with parents and their baby to a place nearby where there are other babies and children, such as a park, playground, or recreation center.
Look around and watch what the babies and children are doing. Point out to the parents how different all the babies are and how they are at different stages of development. Babies do not stay the same. Babies grow and change at different rates and develop skills at different ages. This is normal. It is fun to see how babies change at various ages and how babies are different from one another even at the same age.

Using the charts in the "Babies Change" topic of the *Baby Grows* parent book, talk about what you and the parents can see babies of various ages doing.
Compare what older and younger children are doing to what their baby is doing now. Remind the parents that this isn't to measure how well their baby is doing, but to see what babies do at different stages.

Emphasize that all babies grow, but they grow at different rates.
Parents can use the information in the charts as a general guide to growth and development, but it should not be used as a rigid timetable for growth. If parents are worried about their baby's growth, suggest they talk to their health care provider about their baby.

Charting growth milestones is something parents may enjoy.
Help parents fill out the "Body Changes" chart with the approximate dates their baby did each of these things. These things are records of large and small muscle skills—they involve moving around and holding things in fingers or using feet to kick.

Consider asking if the parents kept a record of their older children's milestones. It can be interesting to compare and contrast sibling development, but remind parents that all children grow and develop at their own rate.

Physical development (large and small muscle skills) is one kind of development. Other kinds of development are emotional (feelings) and intellectual (thinking).

Brainstorm some milestones in emotional (feelings) and intellectual (thinking) development and ask the parents to think back to when their baby first did these things.
Use the baby's name when you ask these questions:

- When did (baby) first cry when a parent left?

- When did (baby) show a special preference for a toy or blankets?

- When did (baby) first say a "word"?

- Has (baby) shown an interest in caring for a baby doll?

Give the parents the crayons and paper and suggest they create a colorful growth chart of their baby's progress.
They can create one page per type of development (emotional, intellectual, small and large muscle) or put all types on one page.

Activity 2: Encouraging Physical Development

Point out to the parents that as we watch our children grow, some of the most obvious changes will be physical.
Talk about the physical changes parents have seen in their child. Not only the changes in weight and size are noticeable, but the ability of their baby to control and coordinate her muscles.

Ask the parents to brainstorm some ideas on helping babies develop physically.
Here are some ideas to share:

- Help your baby turn over. Put your hands on his back and tummy and help him turn.

- Babies like to hang on to their parent's finger. As they get bigger, they like help sitting and standing.

- Babies like to look at and reach for things. Mobiles and crib gyms with lightweight, colorful items encourage baby to reach out and bat at the objects.

- Babies like to move—rock your baby in rocker, move to music, go for a walk with the baby in a front pack or stroller.

Demonstrate how to gently roll the baby on a partially blown-up beach ball.
The baby will enjoy this game and it helps him develop his balance. (Remind parents to be sure to hold onto their baby while he is on the ball.)

Help parents plan playful, physical activities that are appropriate for the age of their baby using the ideas on the Helping Baby Grow Strong handout.
Large muscle activities help a baby develop in several ways beyond the physical. A baby will use problem-solving skills to figure out how to do different actions. She may practice her language skills as she talks about the playing or listens to parents explain and encourage her. A baby and his parents bond even more when they play together.

Ask the parents to look around their home to find some new ways to use household furnishings and objects for play and learning.
Here are some ideas; you will have many more.

- place large pillows from a sofa on the floor for the baby to crawl over

- rearrange furniture so the baby can easily get from one to another

- childproof a kitchen cupboard for the baby to climb in and out of

- surround a low footstool with pillows to jump into

- make a tunnel to crawl through by draping a table or chairs with a blanket

- roll and kick a soft ball

- have dad or mom crawl over and hug the baby

Give the parents the handout and point out how large-muscle play activities can change as a child grows and changes.

Remind the parents to always put safety first.
Help them look at their home and the play ideas to find ways to make sure their child is protected.

Balls of all sizes can encourage large- and small-muscle development. Play with the baby using different kinds of balls. Babies like balls that can be picked up, rolled, kicked, and tossed.

Encourage the parents to use their home in other ways to encourage development. Many household objects can be safely substituted for toys of all kinds.

Closing

Help parents summarize what they learned by going over these points. You may want to add others if you notice parents need more information.

✓ A baby's body is growing and changing all the time.

✓ Parents can observe their babies and record their baby's development.

✓ Parents who carefully observe their baby and learn as much as they can about him will be able to help their baby grow best.

✓ Parents can encourage learning and physical development with simple games and activities they do.

Helping Baby

Discipline

Getting Ready

Agenda

- **Opening:** helping our children grow
- **Keeping It Going:** help for specific stages
- **Closing:** using what we've learned

Objectives

Parents will

- understand that the very first step in learning about guiding and disciplining a young child is to learn about child development
- learn the importance of consistent, loving discipline to help their children learn and grow
- understand that discipline is guiding and teaching a child about the best ways to behave
- start to talk about toilet training and learn the signs that indicate when a child is physically and emotionally ready to be toilet trained
- begin to establish a sleep routine to help their children understand what to expect at bedtime and feel safe and relaxed so parents and child can enjoy bedtime

In Advance

- Review the information in the parenting information book *Baby Grows.*

Materials

Activity 1: What and Why of Discipline

- Young Family Parenting Information book *Baby Grows* for parents
- copy of the poem A Warm Coat in the Winter at the end of this section
- paper
- markers or crayons

Getting Ready (continued)

Activity 2: How to Discipline
- Young Family Parenting Information book *Baby Grows* for parents
- Make a set of cards with various situations that could be considered misbehavior. Include things like pulling a tablecloth off the table, flushing a toothbrush down the toilet, refusing to eat lunch, and other simple things young children do.

Activity 3: Toilet Training
- Young Family Parenting Information book *Baby Grows* for parents
- Several different books about toilet training for children and for parents. The librarian at your local public library can help you find appropriate titles.

Activity 4: Naptime/Bedtime
- child's favorite blanket or other object the child uses for comfort
- Several books appropriate for bedtime reading with children. The librarian at your local public library can help you find appropriate titles.
- recorded quiet music or lullabies and a way to play them

Discipline

Opening

"There are many ways parents help their children. By disciplining with love and consistency, we help our children learn to live in a group and get along with others. Other routines for toilet training and bedtime can also make life go more smoothly for a child and his family as well as make the child feel self-confident and secure."

Keeping It Going

Activity 1: What and Why of Discipline

Acknowledge that discipline means different things to different people, depending on how they were brought up and disciplined by their own parents and others.
It is important to realize the influence of the parents' own families on how they discipline and the influence of their families on how they decide to raise their own children.

Point out that it is up to the parents to teach their children how to behave and live as part of a bigger world with its rules, challenges, and different situations and places.
By teaching their children, parents help their children make decisions that will keep them safe and secure and enable them to live in harmony with others.

Discuss with the parents their ideas about discipline.

- What do they remember about being disciplined?

- How do they plan to discipline their own children?

- Will they change anything from how they were disciplined? What and why?

Continue with questions about what the parents want to learn about discipline from your visits with them.

This is a very big topic and what you cover will depend on the age of the child. Parents have many, many questions about the whats, whys, and hows of discipline. Don't try to cover the entire topic in one visit. Come back to this topic as their child grows and changes.

Remind parents that discipline is not really an issue until a child is 18 months or older. Until then a baby can't understand rules. Even after 18 months, it takes a long time for kids to understand and be able to follow their parents' guidance.

It is important that parents understand what discipline means and why discipline is important. The Young Family series presents discipline as one of the most important responsibilities of parenting.

Parents may differ in what they think discipline does and what they think the most important part of discipline is. That's okay. Encourage them to discuss these differences and work out ways to agree on the importance of discipline and agree on techniques to use. Families need to make a commitment to consistent, loving discipline.

Read the poem A Warm Coat in the Winter to the parents or ask one of them to read it.

The poem can help parents understand the importance of discipline and how it works to keep kids safe. Using the ideas in the poem, talk about how discipline is like a protective coat for a child. Just as parents wouldn't send their children out in the snow without a coat to protect them, they don't want to send their children into the world without the protection that discipline offers.

Discuss with the parents how discipline can protect their children.

What protection does discipline offer? Here are some ideas:

- The child feels safe and secure in unfamiliar situations because he knows rules of behavior.
- The child can get along in a group because she knows the give and take of sharing and getting along with others.
- With the guidelines of discipline, the child can make good decisions about how to behave.
- Limits make a child feel safe and secure.

Ask what else discipline might do for a child and her family.

Activity 2: How to Discipline

Help parents understand that one challenge all parents face is understanding child development and how kids grow.

Very young babies may do things their parents don't like, but it is not misbehaving because they don't understand rules. Between the ages of seven and 24 months, children are beginning to understand rules and learning how to control some of their behaviors.

Ask the parents if they have a challenging behavior they are dealing with now.

Discuss their baby's behavior and some reasons she may be acting this way. Brainstorm some ways the parents could change the situation to improve the problem.

Review why children misbehave.

Use the cards with various situations and discuss with parents whether or not the actions of the child are misbehavior. Then, continue the discussion by asking if the situation would change if the child were older or younger.

Review the different methods of discipline.
The methods a parent uses depends on the age of their child, the situation, and their own philosophy of discipline. Remind parents that before 18 months, the best way to discipline is to change the area to lessen the chances of a child getting in trouble. Put away breakables, keep magazines out of reach, and so forth. Parents can distract or move their child away from the situation, too.

Review each of the situations and discuss the ways to discipline.
Ask parents what other situations they have experienced with their child. How did they discipline then? Did it work?

Continue the discussion by asking parents to suggest alternate methods of discipline that might work in the situations. Ask questions like these:

- Will the first method of discipline you try always work? Why or why not?

- How do you decide which method to try?

- What else might work in this situation? Are there methods that could make this situation worse?

Remind parents that most discipline methods aren't appropriate for very young—pre-18 months—children. Instead, parents should work to understand child development and why kids do what they do, learn how to change the home environment to match each stage, learn their child's temperament, and learn how to adjust their own lives and expectations.

Activity 3: Toilet Training

Acknowledge that toilet training is a big milestone for both parents and their child.
It can only be successful, though, if their child is ready physically and emotionally and if parents offer consistent, loving help during training.

Review the signs of readiness for toilet training in the *Baby Grows* parent book.
If their child is the appropriate age, talk about their child's readiness for toilet training. Which of the signs has he shown? What is yet to come?

Families with more than one child may benefit from a discussion of matching the discipline method to the individual child's temperament, age, and development. Talk about how one method that works with one child may not work with another.

Spanking or other physical punishments are never recommended. These do not get the long-term results that parents want. It may work to change the immediate behavior, but it won't teach a child why he should change this behavior.

Be alert for parents who have unrealistic expectations for toilet training or who punish accidents as a way to train. You may need to spend more time on this with these parents.

Show the parents the books you brought.
Point out the many different methods there are for toilet training. Ask if they have tried any of the methods or know other parents who have. If so, ask questions like these to continue the discussion:

- Did it work? Why or why not?

- Could you change part of the method so it might work?

- What other methods have you heard about?

Discuss which method might work best for their child, based on what they know about their child's temperament, and development and the situation.
If their child is the appropriate age, encourage the parents to share one or more of the children's books about using the toilet with their child.

Discuss how their child reacted to the book.
Was he interested in the book and the idea of toilet training? Or did he seem not to care? What does this tell parents?

Activity 4: Naptime/Bedtime

Begin by asking what the bedtime routine is at this house.

- What steps do parents follow?

- Does the same routine work no matter who puts the child to bed—mom, dad, grandma, babysitter?

Review the reasons routines are important in the *Baby Grows* parent book.

If there is no bedtime routine, brainstorm the parts of a routine with the parents.
Encourage the parents to start the bedtime routine tonight. Talk about what to include, then make a plan to start the routine.

Share the bedtime books with parents, and read them together.
Play the lullabies, too. Would either of these things encourage their child to sleep? Talk about choosing appropriate books and music for bedtime. Parents will want to avoid books and music that stimulate rather than calm and soothe. Dance music, for example, encourages activity. Quiet music encourages sleep.

Ask if the parents have any special concerns about sleep/naptime or if they have any problems with their baby at bedtime.
If they do, go over the suggestions in *Baby Grows* with some ideas to try in different situations. You may want to follow the routine if it is naptime and then discuss ways to make it work with their child.

Before closing, point out how bedtime can be a great family time.
All the children can come together for cuddling and reading. Then each child can have a few minutes of special time with mom and/or dad. As kids get older, bedtime can be a good time to encourage kids to share their thoughts and worries.

"'Sweet dreams' are what parents wish for all of their children. Special love and attention at bedtime can help make dreams and sleep peaceful and restful."

Closing

Help parents summarize what they learned by going over these points. You may want to add others if you notice parents need more information.

- ✓ Discipline is one of the most important responsibilities of parenting.
- ✓ Through consistent, loving discipline, parents help their children become happy, responsible adults.
- ✓ There are many different methods of discipline. Knowing their child and the situation will help parents choose the right methods.
- ✓ Discipline of very young children involves adjusting the home environment and parental expectations.
- ✓ Toilet-training will only work when a child is emotionally and physically ready.
- ✓ Sleep routines make bedtime and naptime go more smoothly because routines give a child a chance to adjust to the transition from play and fun to sleep.

Beware of starting a sleep routine at the "wrong" time of day for a child. You and the parents may find out just how well the routine signals bedtime when the child vigorously resists the signals of the bedtime routine.

Handout

Helping Baby Grow Strong

Play Ideas That Are Fun and Help Baby Grow

The following playful suggestions help babies and toddlers develop large-muscle skills and encourage learning. Pick activities that seem like a good match for your child's interests and abilities while keeping safety in mind. If the ideas seem too tough now, try again in a week or so. You may be surprised at how fast your baby develops. Older preschoolers and toddlers may find these activities exciting when they are done as part of an "obstacle course." Encourage your child with your enthusiasm and interest in their playful efforts to learn and grow. Applaud, laugh, participate, or proudly sit back and watch as your little one gets stronger and smarter everyday!

- Roll your baby on a partially inflated beach ball. Place baby on his stomach on top of a beach ball. Carefully hold onto to him while you gently rock the ball back and forth. (This idea may also be helpful when trying to comfort a crying baby.)

- Encourage your baby to hang onto your fingers and pull herself to a sitting or standing position.

- Put a plaything slightly out-of-reach and encourage your baby to try to get the toy.

- Your baby can drop clothes pins or teaspoons into an open coffee can. To make it more challenging, cut holes slightly larger than the object in the plastic lid.

- Have baby crawl, roll, or walk between two pieces of furniture.

- Arrange some pieces of furniture so baby can easily get from one to the other.

- Put large pillows on the floor for baby to walk or crawl over.

- Put a mattress on the floor for baby to jump on and practice falling.

- Surround a low footstool with a pile of pillows for baby to jump into. Outside, collect a pile of dry leaves for baby to jump into.

- Find or make a "walker" toy which your baby can push ahead of her as she learns to walk. They give a beginning walker support and balance. (A small chair that slides across the floor easily can make a good walker toy.)

- Find or make toys that make sounds: drums to pound, things to shake, xylophones to tap.

- Drape a small table with a blanket for baby to hide or crawl under.

- Encourage baby to try out a toddler-sized slide. They have just a few steps to climb to reach a short slide.

- Have balls of several sizes for baby to throw, kick, or roll.

(continued)

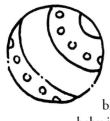

- Blow bubbles to grab for and chase after.

- Place pillows, cushions, or folded blankets on a carpeted floor. Have baby jump from one to another.

- Place large, sturdy cooking pots upside down in a line. Have baby use them as stepping stones.

- Make a tunnel for baby to crawl through with big cardboard boxes or tables covered with blankets.

- Lay a broom flat on the floor. Have baby walk along the broom handle. Or, use a string or rope instead of the broom.

- Prop up one end of a 2" x 8" board (watch for splinters). Make sure it isn't wobbly. Have baby walk up and down the incline.

- Have baby throw "bean bags" into a bucket or basket. (For easy bean bags, fill a clean sock part way with dry rice or beans. Tie it very tight.)

- Encourage new ways of moving—have baby walk or crawl backwards or sideways, turn in a circle, become all loose and wiggly.

- Drape a rope between two chairs. The lowest part of the rope can be as high as 6" to 8" off the floor. Have baby step over the rope. (Don't tie the rope to the chairs. The child could trip and pull the chairs onto himself.)

- Draw circles with chalk on the floor. Or, use hula hoops or string. Have baby jump into and out of the circles, or jump backwards or sideways.

- Set a large laundry basket on its side. Have baby try to kick a ball into the basket.

- Teach baby how to bounce a ball. (Most children won't be able to catch yet. A small, under-inflated beach ball works well for beginners.)

- Have baby peddle a trike.

- And best of all—have mom or dad playfully wrestle with, chase after, crawl over, and hug.

✏ Other Ideas

_____

_____

_____

_____

_____

_____

_____

_____

_____

_____

_____

_____

_____

_____

_____

_____

_____

_____

_____

_____

_____

A Warm Coat in the Winter

by Joe Moses

I want my children to get along with others.
I want them to be able to take care of themselves
and learn how to make decisions.

I want them to be safe
and feel secure.
Because I love them.

But they talk back to me.
They fight.
They scream.
They throw things.
They say, "I hate you."

And sometimes I hate them, too.

So, sometimes I talk back to them.
And fight.
And scream.
And throw things.
And say, "I don't know what else to do."

But I know what I want.

I want them to be proud of themselves,
and respect others.

I can teach my children
by giving them rules,
setting limits,
and catching them doing things I like.

Discipline is like a warm coat in the cold.

My children can put it on themselves
when they need it,
to keep them safe and secure.

They can be proud of it and pass it on.
And they'll know I love them
because I gave them the coat.

Chapter 6
Baby Plays

Introduction

Home Visitor Information

Baby Plays shows parents how they can encourage their baby's physical, intellectual, and emotional development through what many consider to be merely "child's play." Child's play is one of the most important ways children learn about the world around them and where they fit into it. You have the opportunity to help parents see the importance of spending time playing with their baby. You can help them find the time to play, too, by helping them turn daily activities into fun, stimulating play.

Additional activities and information have been added to the *Baby Plays* parenting information book. This will give you more activities to show parents how to play with their baby. You have a great opportunity to show parents different, imaginative ways to play and use household objects and routines in their play. Parent-child play builds bonds and attachment. This is important to the well-being of their baby because it shows her how much her parents care. Encourage the parents to watch their child at play and to join in the play.

After the activities in *Baby Plays*, parents will

- understand that play is important for a child's development
- understand how children's play changes as they grow and play
- develop ideas for playing with their child
- discover how children change in their play as they grow and develop
- be aware of age-appropriate play and toys
- have many ideas of ways to play with their baby
- have ideas for toys and games to play with their children
- know more about homemade and purchased toys
- be encouraged to play with their child through simple games

Important Information for Home Visitors

- Play helps a baby grow and learn about herself, others, and about how the world works. Play may help a baby learn about her ethnic and cultural heritage, too.

- As a baby grows, the way he plays changes. Parents need to watch their baby closely to see how their baby is playing and think about what their baby might be learning.

- Parents can have fun with their baby and get to know him better when they play together.

- When playing with toys, a baby is learning how to use her body. Sometimes a baby will need her parents to show her how to play with toys.

- When babies play with toys, they will often want to do the same things over, and over, and over. They will also like to hold, taste, drop, bang, and throw their playthings.

- Parents don't need to spend a lot of money on toys. Many things in the home can become "toys" and parents can make many other kinds of playthings for their baby.

- Parents need to keep safety in mind for all toys, both store-bought and homemade.

Additional Topic Information

Play Is Important

When we think about childhood, one of the first things we may picture is play. In most cases, children have the opportunity to play with parents and other family members, with toys, and with friends. For many adults, memories of childhood play are greatly treasured.

When children play, they learn many things. Play is not a luxury that only some children can afford. Some people even say that play is a child's work. When they play, children are learning important ideas, behaviors, and skills that they will need in order to live and work as an adult. Even in families where life is very stressful or unsure, children still need the time and the opportunity to play.

If parents understand how children play at different ages and what children learn through their play, they can help their child play. They may be more patient with their child when her play seems frustrating or upsetting to them, too.

As children grow, their play changes. For example, very young babies would rather play with people than with toys or objects. Older babies like to play with both people and toys. Below is a brief description of how children play at different ages and the kinds of things that children are learning when they play.

During the **first month** of life, babies "play" and learn about their world by looking at things. They enjoy looking at faces, bright colors, and simple objects. By looking at and watching people and things, newborns are becoming familiar with the world in which they live.

From **one to four months,** babies explore their bodies to learn what is part of themselves and what is part of the rest of world. They like to do things over and over, like kick or make sounds with their voices. At this age, babies are learning that the world is controllable and predictable.

From **five to eight months,** babies begin to play with objects. Babies play with objects by holding, shaking, tasting, and dropping them. They learn that one thing can cause another thing. For example, by shaking a rattle, a baby learns that shaking causes the rattle to make a noise. Babies at this age begin to play "social" games with others, like peek-a-boo. A baby will even laugh at "jokes" that someone plays, such as tugging at a toy the baby has or pretending to suck on the baby's pacifier or bottle. The baby may even join in the joke by trying to pull out the pacifier or bottle from the other person's mouth.

From **nine to 12 months,** babies are learning about the relationships between objects. They're learning that covers fit on tops of containers, that cups sit on saucers, and that spoons fit in cups. Babies at this age like to hit things together, like two blocks or a spoon and a pan, and are better at using their thumb and first finger to hold objects rather than using their entire hand.

When children are **12 to 18 months old,** they love to copy the people around them. A child will try to get another child her own age to play with her by offering toys or by copying something the other child does. She will make a game of it. Children at this age begin to show an interest in scribbling with crayons and will build things with blocks. They are more aware of themselves as people and may "show off" in front of others to make them laugh. They may show delight in doing something for the first time, like standing up without help or walking.

From **18 to 24 months,** some of a child's play becomes "symbolic." This means that he pretends that one thing is another thing. For example, he may pretend that a block is a car or that his mother's hair is a kitty. This kind of play gives children a sense of control over their world, which sometimes can seem dominated by adults and their demands. This pretend play helps prepare children for more difficult kinds of thinking that they will need to do as older children and adults.

By learning how children play at different ages, parents will learn what kinds of things their child will like to play with and what kinds of toys and games will help their child learn and grow well. No matter what a baby's age, however, her favorite play activity will be to spend time with her parents or others in the family.

The goal of this section is to help parents learn about the importance of play for their baby's growth and development and how parents can play with their baby.

Some parents may have had painful experiences related to play. Some parents may not have been able to play because of severe family circumstances. Some parents may feel that children need to learn at a very young age that life is work and not play. Your visit can be a time for parents to share their feelings about their own childhood play experiences as well as their child's play. They can see that play will be important to their child, too.

Toys and Games

Toys can play an important role in a child's growth and development. When children play with toys, they begin to associate words with objects, learn about the relationships between objects, and learn how some things in the world work. They are beginning to make sense of the world.

Did you ever make toys out of common objects when you were a child? For example, to an adult a wooden spoon is just a wooden spoon. But to a child, a wooden spoon can be a hammer, a drum stick, a magic wand, a person with a long, skinny body, or the key to a giant door.

Parents may be surprised to learn that they probably have many things right in their own home that would be excellent toys for their baby. Parents don't need to spend a lot of money on toys to provide their child with opportunities to play and learn. Sometimes parents will buy an expensive toy only to find that their baby would rather play with the box. Parents may need some reassurance that their child will grow and develop just fine with simple toys, homemade toys, and a clean and safe place in which to play.

Activities in this section will help parents learn what kinds of toys and games their baby will like at different ages and how they can make some of the toys for their baby.

Parents may have some issues around toys. They may have had painful experiences related to toys. Some parents may not have had any toys or only a few because of financial problems in their families. Some parents may have lost a special toy as a child. Others may feel that toys are not necessary at all. Your visit can be a time for parents to share their feelings about their own childhood experiences with toys as well as their feelings as a parent of a young child.

Games, songs, and rhymes are important parts of play, too. A child can take almost any action and make a game out of it, like dropping a spoon on the floor, making a funny noise, or hiding around the corner. Children also love games that others teach them, like peek-a-boo or hide-and-seek. Think about the games that you played as a child. What kinds of games did you play? Did you make up games or did you learn them from other children? Did anyone in your family teach you special songs or rhymes?

Games and songs are often passed from one generation to the next. The words and rhymes might change a bit, but often the games that children know are very similar to the ones their grandparents and even great-grandparents knew. Games and songs are a way for children to learn about their culture and ethnic heritage, too. Songs can teach children about important historical events, specific customs, and beliefs that are highly valued.

Children love games and songs because the words are easy to remember, the actions are simple, and often there is a surprise of some sort. Babies will love to play the same game over, and over, and over. Parents need to remember that babies learn by repeating things. When a baby likes something, she will want to do it many times. If parents keep these things in mind, they may be more patient with their child when she asks for the same game again and again.

All the small things parents and children do together, like playing games, reading books, or saying rhymes, help the children build the basic skills they will need for thinking, learning, and relating to people. You can encourage parents to play with their child, both with and without toys. Remind them that this is a very special and important time in their child's life. The more they play with their child, the better they will know their child and the more they will learn what their child needs to grow and develop to his fullest potential.

Concerns to Be Aware of During Home Visits

If you do notice any of these concerns, discuss them with the parents and/or your supervisor. Your supervisor will help you decide what needs to be done.

- Parents who don't play with their baby.

- Parents who are embarrassed to have fun with their baby.

- Parents who don't think play or toys are important for babies.

- A baby who doesn't seem interested in people or things around him.

- Parents who don't know what kind of toys to give to their baby or who give their baby toys that are meant for much older children and expect their baby to know how to play with them.

- Parents who give their baby toys that are not safe.

Play Is Important

Growing and Learning

Getting Ready _____

Agenda

- **Opening:** play is important
- **Keeping It Going:** what babies learn from play
- **Closing:** using what we've learned

Objectives

Parents will

- understand that play is important for a child's development
- discuss how children's play changes as they grow and play
- develop ideas for playing with their child

In Advance

- Review the information in the parenting information book *Baby Plays*.

Materials

Activity 2: Things to Know About Play

- Young Family Parenting Information book *Baby Plays* for parents
- copy of the Just Playing? handout at the end of this section

Growing and Learning

Opening

"As children grow, their play changes, too. It becomes more involved, more active, more everything. Parents need to understand the importance of play so they can encourage play and provide the opportunity for play for their child."

Keeping It Going

Activity 1: Why Do Children Need to Play

Go over the "Growing and Learning" topic in the *Baby Plays* parent book.

You can point out that play is serious business for kids. It is the way they figure out the world and what things mean—how things work, how people get along, and how they fit in. Play is the way kids have fun, but it is also the way they learn.

Ask the parents some questions like these to spark a discussion:

- Do you have time to play with your child?

- How do you like to play with your child?

- How does playing with your child make you feel? Relaxed, energized, happy, or some other feeling?

Talk with parents about the four different kinds of play.
You can describe play like this:

- Active play: running, biking, throwing, kicking — helps physical development.

- Creative play: drawing, clay play, singing, music making — exercises small motor skills and imagination.

- Imaginative play: dress-up and make believe — encourages problem solving, language development, and helps social-skill development.

- Nurturing play: playing with dolls/stuffed animals — helps kids develop emotionally and understand their feelings and others'.

Even though these activities stress that play is an important part of how children learn, parents shouldn't think of play as "work." Play should be fun for both the parents and their child.

Some parents may have little experience with play—either playing themselves as children or adults—or playing with their children. It may take more talking and demonstrations on how to play to encourage these parents to play. But keep at it. It is worth it to help parents encourage their baby's development through play.

If there are older children in the family, encourage the parents to watch them play, too, and think about how play has helped them learn and grow. It might be easier to see and understand nurturing play when watching a 3-or 4-year-old with a doll than watching an infant.

With the parents, watch their child at play.

Depending on the age of the child, point out the different things the child is doing that fall into the four groups above. Not everything will look like "play."

Help the parents put their child's activities into groups like these:

Active Play

- Ages birth to 3 months — kicking feet, waving hands, wiggling fingers
- Ages 3 to 6 months — lifting head, looking around, grabbing things, crawling
- Ages 6 to 12 months — trying to stand and/or walk
- Ages 12 to 18 months — may ride toy trike, climbing
- Ages 18 to 24 months — starting to run, climb, kick ball, jump

Creative Play

- Ages birth to 3 months — responds to different sounds, songs, bright colors
- Ages 3 to 6 months — starting to "talk" and "sing," make funny sounds
- Ages 6 to 12 months — making noise with objects (pounding on blocks), likes or doesn't like the way different things feel
- Ages 12 to 18 months — stacking blocks (2 or 3), likes musical instruments and, simple puzzles
- Ages 18 to 24 months — scribbling with big crayons on big sheets of paper, stringing big beads, building taller towers

Imaginative Play

- Ages birth to 3 months — likes parent's voice, peek-a-boo
- Ages 3 to 6 months — likes different sounds, watching different people
- Ages 6 to 12 months — copying parents, waving bye
- Ages 12 to 18 months — may play with another child, play simple hide-and-seek or make tents with blanket and table, make mud pies
- Ages 18 to 24 months — starting to play house, care for dolls, go "shopping," dress-up, be an animal

Nurturing Play

- Ages birth to 3 months — likes faces; responds to parent and encourages interaction by smiling, cooing, may have a special blanket or toy

- Ages 3 to 6 months — likes simple interactive games like peek-a-boo, pick up, so big, pat-a-cake

- Ages 6 to 12 months — wants to be like their parents, copy simple things their parent does like kissing, waving, clapping, makes dolls sing or talk

- Ages 12 to 18 months — likes to cuddle when reading with a parent, likes talking to dolls, animals, people

- Ages 18 to 24 months — cares for "babies," acts out scenes/feelings with puppets or dolls

Encourage the parents to choose one of the play types and involve their baby in playing that way.
Discuss the different play styles parents have—what their preferred way to play with their baby is. Some parents will enjoy more active play while others may enjoy reading, doing puzzles, or other quiet play. One type isn't better than another; every child needs to experience all kinds of play.

Activity 2: Things to Know about Play

Go over the information in the *Baby Plays* parent book.
Ask the parents if they have noticed how their child likes to play. Does their child seem to more interested in active play or quiet play? Does she choose to play with trucks over dolls? Each child will have a play style, but all children need to have the chance to try all types of play.

Point out that the purpose of play is to have fun, but the outcome of play is development and learning.
A baby is having fun when he plays with blocks or dolls, but he is learning many different things, too.

Share the information on the Just Playing? handout with the parents.
Keeping in mind the age of the child, play with the baby to show parents how their baby is learning each of these skills or concepts. Where appropriate, use the baby's own toys or things around the house.

Siblings want to play with the baby, too. Talk about how to teach older kids appropriate, gentle ways to involve the baby in play. Remind parents to be sure to supervise play between the baby and her siblings.

Be sure you choose ways to play that are age-appropriate for the baby.

Here are some skills that happen when young (under one year old) babies play:

Problem-solving

- figuring out how to grab a toy that is just out of reach
- figuring out how to get the shapes through the holes of a shape—matching toy
- figuring out how what happens when he manipulates a toy (like a pop-up) to make something happen,

Social Abilities

- "talking" with a parent when the parent talks to him
- "talking" to baby — herself — that she sees in a mirror

Creative Ideas

- using pots and spoons to make noise
- playing peek-a-boo with blanket

Fantasy and Imagination

- playing with dolls
- imitating what parents do

Feelings

- making faces to show different simple emotions—happy, sad, etc.
- taking care of dolls

Knowledge and Concepts

- playing with water in the bathtub, pouring, and splashing
- stacking things on top of one another
- singing songs

Persistence

- trying until he gets it
- doing it again another day

Remind parents that sharing and cooperation and playing with others are skills that come later, around three to four years old. Babies are just beginning to learn to play. They want to play mostly with familiar people like parents and siblings.

Let parents play with their baby with these ideas in mind.
Discuss what you and the parents see while they play with their baby.

Closing

Help parents summarize what they learned by going over these points. You may want to add others if you notice parents need more information.

✓ Playing is the way children learn about the world around them and how they fit into it.

✓ Play is important for children's growth and development.

✓ Parents who understand child's play can provide their children with the kind of play that will help them grow best.

✓ Watching their child play can help parents see what children learn from their play.

✓ There are different ways to play—active, quiet, creative, and others—that all kids enjoy. Some children will show a preference for one type of play over others and may need encouragement to play in all ways to promote their development.

✓ Babies are always learning when they play. Parents can encourage learning by playing with their baby.

✓ Parents who watch their babies and learn as much as they can about them will be able to help their babies grow best.

Playing with Your Baby

Getting Ready _____

Agenda

- **Opening:** how a baby's play changes as he grows
- **Keeping It Going:** toys and other ways to play with your baby
- **Closing:** using what we've learned

Objectives

Parents will

- discover how children change in their play as they grow and develop
- discuss age-appropriate play and toys
- learn many ideas of ways to play with baby

In Advance

- Review the information in the parenting information book *Baby Plays*.

Materials

Activity 1: Play Through the Ages

- Young Family Parenting Information book *Baby Plays* for parents
- some of the items listed as age-appropriate for this child in the "Ideas for Play" charts in the *Baby Plays* parent book
- toy catalogs with pictures and descriptions that include recommended ages

Getting Ready (continued)

Activity 2: Playing Along

- some of the items listed as age-appropriate for this child in the Ideas for Play charts in the *Baby Plays* parent book

- Make a set of Play Idea Activity Cards. Write different types of play on each card. Here are some types of play to include:

  - song or dance

  - puppets or finger plays

  - small motor activity toys

  - make a book or draw a picture

Playing with Your Baby

Opening

"As children grow, their play changes, too. It becomes more involved, more active, more everything. Parents need to understand the importance of play so they can encourage their child to play and to encourage parents to find the opportunity for play."

Remember to encourage a playful attitude, too. Play is fun, not work.

Keeping It Going

Activity 1: Play Through the Ages

Go over the Ideas for Play charts for the appropriate age of the child in the parent book *Baby Plays*.
Talk about which of these ideas the parents have tried. Encourage the parents to use the items you brought to do the activities with their child. If the parents are too shy or reluctant to do it, you can, with the parents' permission, play with the baby. Once you start, encourage the parents to join in.

Talk about the importance of play, describing what parents are doing and how it helps their baby.
Questions like these can help the discussion:

- Which of these activities does your baby seem to like?

- What else have you done that encourages play and learning?

- Have you noticed any changes over the last few weeks in how your baby plays?

Focus on the current age of the child, but look ahead, too, to see how play will change.

Discuss toy safety with parents. Have them look at toys for small parts or ones that might break easily.

Use the pictures from the toy catalog to talk about age-appropriate toys.
Ask the parents why they should follow age recommendations on toys. Here are some reasons to share:

- toys that may have small parts are dangerous to younger children

- a toy that is too complicated can frustrate and discourage a child

- toys that are too difficult to take apart or put together (like Legos) can be frustrating, too, until the child has the skills to use the toys

- some toys may be too big to handle safely—bikes and riding toys can fit this category

Continue by reviewing some toys.
Discuss what makes a good toy for certain ages. Point out how well-designed toys can enhance development. They challenge a baby to figure out how to make it work, the toy can be, or do more, than one thing, or it can spark the imagination.

Activity 2: Playing Along

Tell the parents that it is normal to run out of ideas of ways to play with children.
Both parents and children can benefit from new ideas.

Brainstorm with parents some ways to play with their baby.
Here are a few ideas:

Birth to 6 months old

- let the baby use her parent's body as a climbing hill

- give the baby a gentle "horse ride" on your feet

- make silly faces

- make different noises

- read picture books

- put a blanket over the baby's head, act surprised, and clap when he pulls it off

6 to 12 months old

- take turns tossing bean bags into a box

- hold the baby when you swing or slide down a slide

- let the baby "paint" on his high chair tray with yogurt

- read books together

- let the baby pull off strips of masking tape stuck to a table

- poke holes in the lid of a plastic bottle, fill the bottle with water, and show the baby how to make it "rain"

- sing and dance with the baby
- play follow-the-leader with simple actions

1 to 3 years old
- make a tunnel with empty boxes
- kick a large ball back and forth
- have containers to fill and empty with water, sand, rice, or beans
- give the child a purse or tote and things to put in it
- sort objects into groups by color, size, type, and shape
- use puppets to act out daily activities or to have conversations
- make a matching game with pictures from magazines
- explore the outside world on a walk
- don't forget books!

3 to 5 years old
- play "Simon Says"
- move in different ways — hop, jump, walk backwards
- find things to build with — milk cartons, blocks
- try art projects like collages of pictures
- "paint" the house or sidewalk with water and brush
- play dress-up with old clothes and shoes
- make up tongue twisters
- play board games with simple rules
- start a collection — leaves, rocks, bugs
- read, read, read!

Try some of the activities and games the parents suggested.

Remind the parents that "play" can take place anytime or anywhere; it isn't limited to a set time or to using toys.
Everyday activities can be opportunities for play, too. Talk to the parents about making everyday activities time for fun and learning.

Brainstorm some activities that can be turned into play.
Activities like bathtime, getting dressed, doing laundry, waiting for the bus—just about any time parents and their child are together can be a time to play.

Using the Play-Idea Activity Cards, play a game with the parents.
Take turns choosing a card and using the play idea to make a daily routine fun. For example, you or the parents could make up a silly bathtime song. Leave the set of cards with the parents so they can use them to spark ideas of how to play with their child.

You can easily include older children in the "making routines fun" game. Preschoolers are enthusiastic players and will enjoy getting involved with the baby or creating their own fun routines.

After you and the parents have played the game, involve the child in a game using one of the daily routines, like putting on shoes or changing a diaper.
Ask the parents to turn the routine into a game. Encourage the parents to make the routine fun by playing with their child while they do the chore.

Closing

Help parents summarize what they learned by going over these points. You may want to add others if you notice parents need more information.

- ✓ As babies grow, the way they play changes. Parents change the way they play with their children, too.
- ✓ Play can take place anytime and anywhere if parents make the effort.
- ✓ Daily routines can be part of playtime, too, if parents try to turn the routine into a fun activity.
- ✓ No matter how old a child is, she will still like to play with her mother, father, and other family members best.
- ✓ Play should be fun for a child and his parents.

Toys and Games

Toys and Games

Getting Ready

Agenda

- **Opening:** new ideas for play
- **Keeping It Going:** homemade and purchased toys
- **Closing:** using what we've learned

Objectives

Parents will

- learn some ideas for toys and games to play with their children
- talk about homemade and purchased toys
- be encouraged to play with their child through simple games

In Advance

- Review the information in the parenting information book *Baby Plays*.
- Plan a trip to the local library.

Materials

Activity 1: Toy Ideas By Age

- Young Family Parenting Information book *Baby Plays* for parents
- toy catalogs with lots of pictures (Try to find one with "educational" toys, too.)

Activity 2: Toys You Can Make

- Young Family Parenting Information book *Baby Plays* for parents
- supplies to make one or more of the toys in the parent book
- other supplies or objects that can be turned into safe homemade toys

Getting Ready (continued)

Activity 3: Games to Play

- Young Family Parenting Information book *Baby Plays* for parents
- books/tapes/CDs with games/rhymes from the library or other source

  Some titles to look for:

  - *Finger Rhymes, Hand Rhymes, Play Rhyme,* and *Party Rhymes* all by Marc Brown (note that *Hand Rhymes* and *Play Rhymes* are also available on video)
  - *Clap Your Hands* by Lorinda Bryan Cauley
  - The *Lap Time Song* and *Play Book* by Jane Yolen
  - *Everything Grows* by Raffi (or any Raffi recording)

- Books with simple stories to act out like *Caps for Sale* by Esphyr Slobodkina, *All Fall Down* by Helen Oxenbury, *Five Little Monkeys Sitting in a Tree* by Eileen Christolow, *Wheels on the Bus* by Maryann Kovalski, and any others you know. Your librarian will help you find other books.

Toys and Games

Opening

"Playing is the way kids learn. Infants are learning about their bodies when they play with their fingers and toes. They are learning about their world when they smile and others smile back. As children grow, their play changes, too. It becomes more involved, more active, more everything. Parents need to understand the importance of play so they can encourage play and provide the opportunity for play."

Keeping It Going

Activity 1: Activities to Try

Discuss the "Toy Ideas" topic by age in the *Baby Grows* parent book, focusing on the age of the parents' child.
Talk about how their child plays with the toys, which ones she likes, which ones don't interest her. What is her favorite toy now?

Do a toy survey.
With the parents' permission, empty out the toy box or wherever toys are kept. Look at each toy and talk about it. Suggest that the parents divide the toys into groups based on their child's interest in the toy. Is it interesting to look at? Does their child like it? Is it safe? Is it age-appropriate? How do they rate the playability of the toy—will it hold the interest of their child over a long period and grow with the child? Does it encourage imagination or does the toy do it all for the child?

Ask the parents what toys they would recommend to others and why.
Are there any toys they would give away or discard? Of the toys they have, which do they give the highest rating?

Ask the parents how they decide what toys they buy.
Acknowledge that deciding which toys their child might like can be tough for parents. Look in the toy catalogs at the toys listed for their child's age.

Be sure to compliment parents on any unusual, interesting, or homemade toys.

This may be a chance for parents to pass on toys no longer played with and a chance to look for broken toys to discard.

Parents may feel a lot of pressure to provide their babies and toddlers with many toys. Parents may need reassurance that children will grow and develop just fine with simple toys, homemade toys, and a clean, safe place to play. Young children especially don't need a lot of purchased toys nor do they usually want the latest "hot" toy. It is adults who create the frenzy for the latest hot toy.

Based on what you and the parents learned from the toy survey, discuss the toys in the catalogs.

Are any "necessary"? Which would the child like? Are there homemade or simpler versions of such a toy? What about the "educational" toys—those actually designed to teach something? Do the parents think these toys do what they claim? Continue by asking what the parents look for when buying a toy.

Activity 2: Toys You Can Make

Ask the parents if they have made any toys for their child or if anyone has given them any homemade toys.

If they have some homemade toys, look these toys over and discuss what makes it a good—or not so good—toy.

Share the ideas for homemade toys.

Have the parents tried any of these? Have they made any other homemade toys? What kind?

Using your supplies, help the parents make one of the toys.

Then, get out the other supplies and encourage them to use their imaginations to create another homemade toy.

Be toy inventors!

With the parent's permission, explore their kitchen and other rooms for things that might be used as toys. For example, pots and pans can be noisemakers or hats. For older kids, dry beans can be counted, shoveled like sand, put into an oatmeal box and shaken like a rattle. Scarves or towels can be capes or doll blankets or bandages for "broken" arms. Blankets can turn a table into a cave or tent. Empty margarine tubs can hold water, be floated like boats, and stacked up. The lids can be sailed like a Frisbee. Shaving cream can be colored with food coloring and squished in lots of ways. Toilet paper tubes can be binoculars or megaphones or cut into smaller tubes to string. Milk cartons can be stacked like blocks or made into houses for little people.

Be sure to discuss how appropriate each idea is for the age of their child.

Include a discussion of safety issues, too, such as whether their child would put the shaving cream in his mouth or the beans up her nose!

Keep toy safety in mind whenever making homemade toys. Use nontoxic glues and paints, avoid sharp edges and things small enough to be swallowed.

Creating a safe place to play is discussed in the Young Family Parenting Information book *Safe Child and Emergencies*.

Activity 3: Games to Play

With the parents and child, play the games described in the *Baby Plays* parent book.

What other games do parents and their baby play together?

Show the parents the books with the finger games and rhymes.

Together, figure out how to do the finger motions. Some books may have the music for the rhymes, but don't worry if you and the parents can't read the music. Make up a melody or rhythm that fits the beat of the words. Then play the game with their baby, helping her move her fingers and hands.

Remind the parents that it is not important to get it all right, but to have fun playing and singing with their baby.

As she gets older, the child will be able to do the motions for *Eensy Weensy Spider* or other old favorites. Now, she will enjoy the rhymes and playing with her parents.

Point out that the parents and their child can act out almost any story or book.

There are many books and stories that have fun parts for toddlers to act out.

Read parts of the books you brought so the parents and their child can act it out.

For example, everyone likes the part of *Caps for Sale*, when the peddler stamps his foot and throws his cap on the ground and says, "You monkeys, you give me back my caps!" Do what the monkeys do—stamp your feet and toss your caps on the ground! Talk about ways to involve kids in the story and expand it. What else might monkeys imitate? (This book is also fun to use when illustrating the power of role-modeling appropriate behavior for our children.)

Take a field trip to the local public library to open a world of fun for the parents and their child.

Consider inviting another family along on your field trip to help build networking and support opportunities for both families. If possible, schedule the visit when an age-appropriate story hour or activity is taking place. If that doesn't work, go to the library and help the parents and their child find books, CDs, and tapes; play with the stuff in the library (many children's libraries have dolls, puzzles, and toys to play with); and sign up for a library card. Remind parents that reading to a child is a great way to encourage parent/child interaction.

Many libraries have summer reading programs to encourage children to read. For pre-readers, parents are encouraged to read to their children. Encourage the parents to take advantage of these programs and to get to know their local librarian and library resources.

As with all stories and rhymes that are handed down, there are no "right" ways to say or do these rhymes. If the parents have learned different words or actions to a rhyme, that's great because it enriches all of us to learn different versions of familiar stories. The parents can hand down their version to their child, just as their family perhaps handed it down to them.

Help parents set up a system to keep track of materials borrowed from the library. For example, put the books back in a canvas bag when done reading them, or mark the date due on the calendar. Many libraries now give borrowers a printed list of the books checked out. Put the list in a place to remind you when to return the books.

Closing

Help parents summarize what they learned by going over these points. You may want to add others if you notice parents need more information.

✓ Toys are a big part of every child's play. Knowing what makes a good toy helps parents narrow down the choices from the thousands of toys out there.

✓ The more a toy does for a child, the more the toy may limit the child's imagination and resourcefulness.

✓ Not all good toys come from the store. There are good toys parents can make. Many things found in most households encourage play and imagination, too.

✓ No matter a child's age, his favorite thing is to play with a parent or other loved one. Playing finger games, acting out stories, and singing silly songs are all fun. Young children love games that have simple actions and that repeat things over and over. As babies get older, they like games that have surprises.

✓ The public library and children's librarians are a good source for stories and games to share with our children.

Handout

Just Playing?

For kids, the purpose of play is to have fun and do interesting things. The result of play is development and learning. Here are some skills that happen when kids play. Babies will react and play with parents and siblings. One-year-olds will be just beginning to do a few of these activities, older preschoolers may be doing even more in their play.

Skill: Problem Solving

- tries to get to an out-of-reach toy
- shakes rattle to make noise
- matches colors or shapes in puzzles or games
- builds with blocks, boxes, and more
- learns to make things move, turn, open, etc.
- untangles something, fits pieces together, gets clothes on

Skill: Social Abilities

- talks back when parent "talks"
- makes faces in mirror
- talks or babbles about the things around them, listens when another talks
- finds ways to play, take turns, and cooperate with another

Skill: Imagination

- imitates what parent does—waves arms, makes face
- responds to music and songs
- acts out part of daily life—makes dinner, reads the newspaper, rides on the bus
- works through problems by acting them out— maybe a teddy bear gets comforted about a scary situation or gets scolded for a "no-no"
- makes up stories, songs, rhymes
- includes others in their "let's pretend" play
- uses props in imaginative play (dress-up clothes, toy phone, etc.)

Skill: Feelings

- recognizes parents' feelings by noticing changes in parents facial expressions and tone of voice
- tells another child or adult her feelings—uses words and/or body language
- recognizes others' feelings—"She's sad, her mom left"
- acts out discipline situations, for example, gives a doll a time-out
- comforts others—children, adults, dolls, pets
- takes care of dolls and stuffed animals—feeding, clothing, comforting

Skill: Knowledge and Concepts

- enjoys playing "peek-a-boo" or games where a toy or person is covered with a blanket—"Where's daddy? Here I am!" Baby is learning that things still exist even if he can't see them. This is called object permanence and is an important skill to learn
- uses stacking cups or other things to understand size, volume, etc. in water play or sandbox play
- remembers from previous tries that something will or will not work
- learns the words to songs, rhymes, stories
- remembers routines used in activities—first, put down newspapers, then paint the picture

- dances, sings, makes funny noises

(continued)

Skill: Creative Ideas

- uses one thing for something else—a cooking pot becomes a drum, a crayon a baby doll's bottle, your shoe a truck
- uses paint, crayons, markers, playdough
- enjoys changing the world into something else— making a house out of blankets and a table, calling the sofa a boat while the floor becomes the water
- uses household stuff in play—empty boxes, spoons, pans, spools

Skill: Persistence

- keeps trying to reach a hanging mobile or toy
- enjoys the process of trying to build a tower or put together a puzzle in spite of some failure or frustration
- doesn't get something the first time—willing to try again another day
- has fun while trying (and trying!) to learn new large-muscle skills — jumping, trike or bike riding, tossing or kicking a ball

Meld
parenting that works

Qty.	Title	$ Each	Total
	Young Family at Home	$50.00	

Order Form

Subtotal _____

Shipping & handling _____

MN residents add 6.5% sales tax* _____

Total _____

*Tax exempt #: _____

Shipping & Handling

For orders subtotaling:

Up to $25	$5.00
$25.01 to $75	$7.00
$75.01 to $150	$9.00
Over $150	8% of subtotal

Please call for Air Delivery Services and International Delivery pricing.

All orders must be prepaid.

Most orders are shipped within 2 days from receipt of order (7 to 9 delivery days).

Call for quantity discounts!

Send book(s) to:

Name _____

Agency _____

Street address _____

City _____

State _____ Zip _____

Telephone _____

Email _____

Method of Payment:

☐ Check or money order payable to Meld

☐ Visa   ☐ MasterCard   ☐ American Express

Account No. _____

Exp. Date _____

Signature _____

Mail to:
Meld • 219 North Second Street • Suite 200
Minneapolis, MN 55401

You can also order by phone, fax or on our website!

612-332-7563   612-344-1959 (fax)   www.meld.org